ETERNAL SLAVES

So Choose Your Master Wisely!

John R. Drews

WESTBOW
PRESS®
A DIVISION OF THOMAS NELSON
& ZONDERVAN

All Scriptures in this publication are from the THE HOLY BIBLE, NEW INTERNATIONAL
VERSION®, NIV® Copyright © 1973, 1978, 1984, 2011 by Biblica, Inc.®
Used by permission. All rights reserved worldwide.

WestBow Press books may be ordered through booksellers or by contacting:

WestBow Press
A Division of Thomas Nelson & Zondervan
1663 Liberty Drive
Bloomington, IN 47403
www.westbowpress.com
1 (866) 928-1240

ISBN: 978-1-5127-0130-2 (sc)
ISBN: 978-1-5127-0131-9 (e)

Library of Congress Control Number: 2015911437

Print information available on the last page.

WestBow Press rev. date: 07/28/2015

TABLE OF CONTENTS

LETTER OF INTRODUCTION

Greetings from Libby, Montana! My name is John Drews, and I am a born again follower of Jesus Christ. I'm writing this letter in hopes that you might come to a deeper understanding of where you are today in your spiritual life, or in some cases, spiritual death. It is God's hope that all would come to Him, but many will not. My hope is that by sharing what I have learned, you, the reader, might come to realize where you stand with God, and that you would be drawn to read the Bible, the inspired Word of God. Only Jesus saves, but first you must realize you are lost, in need of a Savior.

Because so many people are busy these days, most don't take the time to read the Bible on a daily basis, and some never do. Knowing this, what I have done is organized key Scriptures on important topics so you have some understanding of the life which you have missed or perhaps misunderstood.

To those of you who live day to day without the Spirit, the Bible says Scripture makes no sense. To you, I've taken the time to explain what the truth is talking about. Many will have some understanding already, but still lack the power to overcome the world. To those, I attempt to encourage each reader to examine their own hearts to make sure they have not been deceived, either by others or by themselves. God may open your eyes, but you may choose to look in the wrong direction. He may give you ears to hear, but you may choose to hear the wrong messages.

But it gets better, or so I say. If we believe what God tells us to believe and we make peace with God, we become eternal slaves to righteousness. Because we believe, we do the will of God, through trials and tribulations, until He takes us to our eternal home in heaven.

The choice then, is not between free or slave; we are slaves. The choice is whom do you serve? Satan is the prince of earth; the father of all lies; the prince of darkness; the deceiver. God the Creator is in heaven; King of kings; Lord of lords; He is Spirit; He is love; He is light. If you choose Him as your master, you become slave to righteousness; a new creation; with eternal hope. Death has no hold on you. If you don't choose wisely, death remains on you and you will never be spiritually alive; thus, the second death. Are you interested in hearing more?

So then, there will be 13 chapters to discuss God's Word. First, we must know who the Creator God is before we can believe in Him with all our heart, soul, mind and strength. God is alive; He has revealed Himself as Three Persons in one so we might know Him in a personal way. He has a plan and purpose for your life, but you must choose to find it. So first, identify who He is!

From there, we learn what He expects from us, and then, after counting the costs, we choose our master. And to the believer, simply be reminded of what God has done for us and rejoice in your hope of eternal life. After reading this book, simply share it with someone you want to see come to a deeper understanding of a relationship with God.

About the cover: As Americans, we think we are born free, as free as the wind blows, and that we have the right to choose where we live, how we live, if we live, and a multitude of other freedoms, of which freedom of religion is included. And we have books, Declarations of Independence and laws on record to prove our position. Even our country's history has roots in trusting God.

God has books also, and one of His books is called *The Bible*, and this book has more importance to each of us than all the books of the world combined. And yet, people ignore what it says and think they are free. Free implies there is no cost, but I suggest there are costs. In fact, our freedom today came at the cost of many deaths in our historic past, and more wars may come again!

In the same way, God teaches us to be aware of the spiritual condition of our soul. We do not choose our sinful nature; Adam and Eve made that choice for us all and we inherited that condition through his blood. We are alive in our flesh, but spiritually dead; therefore, separated from God because of sin. We have no choice, we are born slave to sin; and the punishment for sin is death. But God has an escape for us ... interested yet?

It's a good story, and I love telling it! And since I have experienced both death and life, I can tell you that life is eternally better! That's the good news that this book is written to encourage you with.

There will be Scriptures used; they are absolutely true. If my comments seem incomplete or shallow, they may be, because God is still working on me daily, but I can testify to what God has revealed to me so far; and I do. The stories are fiction, which means they are not real, but written to help those without the Spirit to understand what Scripture is saying. The names I use do not reflect the names of people I actually know. The poetry is given to express truth in a rhyming manner. The poetry is a gift from God, and all I do is write it down. If you don't like it, you won't offend me. If you do enjoy it, praise God for what He has revealed to you.

And thanks be to Bonnie, my wife, who did the spelling corrections, typing and grammar corrections. If she hadn't, your reading would have been difficult!

John R Drews

TELLING HIS STORY

I have come to tell a story, will you take the time to hear?
Will you understand His glory, if I make His message clear?
He will come to save His people; He brings joy into your heart,
He is faithful and forgiving; you must ask Him when to start.

If you're honest and you're willing and are ready for a change,
You can put your trust in Jesus, and your life He'll rearrange.
This takes more than just commitment; there's a book that must be read,
If you want to know His meaning; you must know what has been said.

You must recognize a sinner; you must want repentance too,
You must know God and His glory, and what Jesus did for you.
You must ask for God's forgiveness, you must walk away from sin,
If you seek a holy vision, soon a new life will begin.

When His grace has been accepted, and His Spirit comes your way,
You will understand His story, and what a joy it is to pray.
You will grow in all directions; He will be your only guide,
You will stand as light in darkness; you'll have Jesus on your side.

This is only the beginning; all the rest is up to you,
I have shared with you this message, now there's "things" you must do.
Focus now on Jesus; speak your heart; He's at the door,
It's your personal commitment, that our Lord is looking for.

TESTIMONY POEM OF JOHN DREWS

I wandered in darkness for forty-plus years,
Alone in the crowd where I hid from my fears.
My ambitions obsessed me, the money came fast,
I was king of the mountain; with power, at last!

But oh, what a blunder; a fool I became,
The love that I wanted; my money couldn't claim.
The sins that amused me; in body and mind,
Had made me unhappy, unrighteous; unkind.

Then in walked a trucker, a kind man indeed,
Who looked at my face and saw questions and need.
He said "Buy a Bible", and seek out the truth,
Deception had started way back in my youth.

The rest is now history; the book I did read,
Within it I found every answer and need.
And yes, I repented I've turned toward the light,
I accepted forgiveness; I pray day and night.

I won't slay the devil; for it's not my place,
What fear he must feel; when he looks in my face.
I know I surprised him, like a thief in the night,
The Spirit, now in me, has shown me the light.

Oh God, let me love You; and Jesus, Your Son,
I pray You will teach me, now that we are one.
My life You have started; Your will shall provide,
My heart I surrender; teach me to abide.

FOR BONNIE

All my life, I've been searching for someone,
Someone special to hold me at night,
When I'm ready, I know God will send her,
When I meet her, my heart will delight.

Because my Lord is always faithful,
And His timing is always right,
He has sent to me a woman,
Bringing to me much delight.

I surrender my life to serve Jesus,
He brought purpose and joy to my life,
I am thankful beyond comprehension,
I am thankful for Bonnie, my wife.

She is everything I've ever prayed for,
I will always be faithful and true,
I will love her with all Jesus gives me,
I will trust her in all that we do.

I'm excited just thinking about her,
I can't wait to be held in her arms,
In my eyes I will show my devotion,
On her lips I'll share unspoken charms.

I look forward to making her happy,
May old memories be lost in our past,
With each day comes another beginning,
May our lives bring Him glory at last.

MISSION TIME FOR JOHN DREWS

Have Truth, will travel, this man's card said,
So I called on his number; got into his head.
I heard he liked Bibles, and wrote now and then,
Does he know where he's going, or where he has been?

I believe what he's writing, I have faith all is true,
In fact, as you read this, he's writing to you!
Yep! John is this person, with God in his heart,
On a mission of passion, and I'm anxious to start!

For now, I'm in Libby, but my goal is the world,
There's souls to be saving, from where Satan is hurled.
I've a prayer group behind me, each step of the way,
Our "We Team" is moving, and we're stronger each day.

This is my way to thank you, for prayers and support,
Without you behind me, I'd surely fall short.
Together, our mission; at home and abroad,
The good news of Jesus, and to glorify God.

TOGETHER WITH BONNIE

When you look in my eyes, do you see my devotion?
Do you see what I feel, and respond with emotion?
Because I gave you my heart; it doesn't mean you can break it,
Though I offer my love; it doesn't mean you will take it.

Do you still seek my face, when you're ornery inside?
Can you accept my embrace, when your requests have been denied?
Can you sit and be still, when you're raging inside?
Have you patience with me, in those moments of pride?

Do you grow in your faith, as self centeredness dies?
Can you let foolishness sleep, when awakened by the wise?
Do you lower your guard, when your spirits are high?
Do you catch what I say, when my words pass you by?

Do you hear how I feel, when you see me at rest?
Are you filled with my joy, or are those moments depressed?
Can you see that I'm rich, though some think I'm poor?
Can you see that a little, can prove to be more?

When you think I'm weak, I may still be strong.
When you notice mistakes, it doesn't mean I'm all wrong.
Even when I fall short, I can hold my head high.
Even though I have no wings, both you and I can fly.

So here we are again, together, you and I.
Caught up in our love, watching time go by.
I love you more each day, I know you love me too.
Together we will live, no matter what we do.

Chapter 1
THE TRINITY
GOD THE FATHER; GOD THE SON; GOD THE HOLY SPIRIT

If a person, like myself, wants to talk and write about God, the first thing established should be identifying which God I'm talking about! The big "G" God: the One, the Only! Before I can convince anyone that the Bible is the revealed Truth from God, a person must believe that God exists. You must study and know His attributes and believe He is who HE says He is! Learn about grace. Learn about God's love. Learn what faith is and how God will use these things to then draw you to himself, Seek and you will find!

> I Corinthians 2:14 – *"The man without the Spirit does not accept the things that come from the Spirit of God, for they are foolishness to him, and he cannot understand them, because they are spiritually discerned."* (NIV)

> Proverbs 9:10 – *"The fear of the Lord is the beginning of wisdom, and knowledge of the Holy One is understanding."*

So, I, being a man that God created, will not be able to explain God, the Creator. But what I can do is help you see God by pointing to Him in the ways He has chosen to reveal Himself to us.

> 2 Timothy 3:16 says, *"All Scripture is God-breathed and is useful for teaching, rebuking, correcting and training in righteousness."*

So here we begin to see how God chose to reveal Himself so we might know Him and choose to love Him. Using the Bible to establish that there is only one true God is just the beginning, and then we can learn from all three persons revealed in this Godhead, to grow in our knowledge of Him, our God.

So, God the Father.
> The first line of the Bible is Genesis 1:1 – *"In the beginning God created the heavens and the earth."*

> In Isaiah 43:10-11, the Bible says, *"...before Me no god was formed, nor will there be one after Me. I, even, I am the Lord, and apart from Me there is no savior."*

In Isaiah 44:6, the Bible says, *"This is what the Lord says – Israel's King and Redeemer, the Lord Almighty: I am the first and I am the last; apart from Me there is no god."*

In Isaiah 44:8, the Bible says, *"Do not tremble, do not be afraid. Did I not proclaim this and foretell it long ago? You are my witnesses. Is there any God besides Me? No, there is no other Rock; I know not one."*

In Isaiah 45:5-6, the Bible says, *"I am the Lord, and there is no other; apart from Me there is no god. I will strengthen you, though you have not acknowledged Me, so that from the rising of the sun to the place of its setting men may know there is none besides Me. I am the Lord, and there is no other."*

In John 17:3, the Bible says, *"Now this is eternal life; that they may know You, the only true God, and Jesus Christ, whom You have sent."*

In 1 Corinthians 8:5-6, the Bible says, *"For even if there are so-called gods, whether in heaven or on earth (as indeed there are many "gods" and many "lords"), yet for us there is but one God, the Father, from whom all things came and for whom we live; and there is but one Lord, Jesus Christ, through whom all things came and through whom we live."*

In Galatians 4:8-9, the Bible says, *"Formerly, when you did not know God, you were slaves to those who by nature are not gods. But now that you know God – or rather are known by God – how is it that you are turning back to those weak and miserable principles? Do you wish to be enslaved by them all over again?"*

All these verses have something in common, they describe God the Father. Most seekers and religious people can agree there is only one Creator God, and that He is our Heavenly Father.

So now we know who the Father is, but God revealed Himself to us as three different, equal, powerful persons. God the Father was the first person, with deity, power, uniqueness and oneness. Later we will look at Scriptures that identify all three revealed as one. But for now, believe that the Father exists; is alive; is Spirit; is love and endless other truths. My goal is to steer you towards Him, the one true God; therefore; I must continue to show you Scriptures identifying the fullness of God.

There is no substitute for reading the entire Bible so that He can reveal all His truth to you, but until then, we'll read together a few passages that clearly reveal who God is.

So, let's focus our study on the second person of the triune God, The Son. All religious people who read the Bible or watch religious movies or listen to Christian radio have heard about Jesus, the only begotten Son of God. The Old Testament prophesy pointed to Jesus, the story of the cross and imminent return as He gathers His church.

What many fail to see is His deity; His authority; His perfect obedience to God the Father; His perfect sinless life, which is equivalent to God. Only God is perfect. The Bible says that all have sinned and are not good enough for God's glory. But Jesus, being 100% God and 100% Man, is the only exception in the history of mankind.

> In John 5:19, the Bible says, *"Jesus gave them this answer: 'I tell you the truth, the Son can do nothing by Himself; He can do only what He sees His Father doing, because whatever the Father does the Son also does.'"*

The Father God is perfect by His nature and Jesus did only what God did, making Him perfect. Since only God is perfect and since there is only one True God, you must realize Jesus is God! God Himself revealed Himself to the world He created so that we, His people, could see in Jesus what we could not see in God, the Spirit.

> In John 14:9, *"Jesus answered: 'Don't you know Me, Philip, even after I have been among you such a long time? Anyone who has seen Me has seen the Father. How can you say, 'Show us the Father'?'"*

> In John 14:10-11, the Bible says, *"Don't you believe that I am in the Father, and the Father is in Me? The words I say to you are not just My own. Rather, it is the Father, living in Me, who is doing the work. Believe Me when I say that I am in the Father and the Father is in Me; or at least believe on the evidence of the miracles themselves."*

Jesus is saying to His disciples that He is God in the flesh! God is saying the same thing today! Exercise your faith and believe the truths that God has revealed to us in His word are sufficient to lead us to eternal life.

> I like what the Bible says in John 5:22-23, *"Moreover, the Father judges no one, but has entrusted all judgment to the Son, that all may honor the Son just as they honor the Father. He who does not honor the Son does not honor the Father, who sent Him."*

> In Psalm 50:6, the Bible says, *"And the heavens proclaim His righteousness, for God Himself is judge."*

> In Ecclesiastes 3:17, the Bible says, *"I thought in my heart, 'God will bring to judgment both the righteous and the wicked, for there will be a time for every activity, a time for every deed.'"*

> In Hebrews 12:23, the Bible says *"...You have come to God, the Judge of all men..."*

The Son, Jesus, is the only judge. Many verses say God will judge. Conclusion: Jesus is God! You don't have to explain the unexplainable Creator God; just have faith that He knows what He is doing and He knows why He revealed Himself in the person of Jesus. Obey and believe that all of Scripture is from God and God will reveal more to you as your faith grows.

So, let's grow you faith more as we search for more knowledge concerning God. Let's see what God has revealed to us in His word about the third person in the Trinity of God; God the Holy Spirit.

> Remember how the first line of the Bible in Genesis 1 said, *"In the beginning God created the heavens and the earth."*

Well, in the second verse, God reveals His Holy Spirit.
> Genesis 1:2 says, *"Now the earth was formless and empty, darkness was over the surface of the deep, and the Spirit of God was hovering over the waters."*

God sent His Spirit to move over the water, so God's Spirit can move and it can be sent!
> In Acts 13:2, the Bible says, *"While they were worshipping the Lord and fasting, the Holy Spirit said, 'Set apart for Me Barnabas and Saul for the work to which I have called them.'"*

So, the Holy Spirit speaks!
> In John 16:13, the Bible says, *"But when He, the Spirit of truth, comes, He will guide you into all truth. He will not speak on His own; He will speak only what He hears, and He will tell you what is yet to come."*

> And John 16:15 says, *"All that belongs to the Father is Mine. That is why I said the Spirit will take from what is Mine and make it known to you."*

So, the Holy Spirit is a "He", so a real person who also hears! He tells us the will of Jesus, which is also the will of the Father, which all three together, in harmony, make up the Creator of all things, God.

Now you can understand what the Bible says in John 14:26, *"But the Counselor, the Holy Spirit, whom the Father will send in My name, will teach you all things and will remind you of everything I have said to you."*

This Helper is the Holy Spirit whom the Father will send in His name. Some say the Holy Spirit is only a force, not a person. But the Bible clearly says God sent "Him" and "He" can move on His own, but only does what God tells Him to do. He speaks to us; He lives in us; He hears God and knows God and is God.

We'll talk more about the Holy Spirit later, but as you read the Bible, watch for verses that refer to Him. He is also called Counselor; Holy One; Spirit of Life; Spirit of Truth and Voice of the Lord to mention a few.

Can you now begin to see how all three take on the attributes of the One and only God? Since Scripture never contradicts itself, they must be one and the same! All God, but revealed to seekers in three different ways so we might come to love and understand God on a level that humans can comprehend. Until the day Jesus returns, we have enough information to lead us to God, where His chosen will live forever with Him.

Now that we have a picture of who God is as ONE, and how He looks as three, let's pick some attributes of God, and see how all three work together perfectly as one. As we look at more Scriptures to clarify who God is, take time to review the verses we have already read. Open your Bible and read the whole chapters which are quoted. Don't ever be deceived by those who take Scripture out of context! Take all verses and read them side-by-side to see the fullness of what God's Word is saying.

In Philippians 1:2, the Bible says, *"Grace and peace to you from God our Father and the Lord Jesus Christ."*

Paul is writing a letter to the believers in Philippi and refers to God as Father. In John 1:1-3, the Bible says, *"In the beginning there was the Word, and the Word was with God, and the Word was God. He was with God in the beginning. Through Him all things were made; without Him nothing was made that has been made."*

Jesus is the Word, known also as the Bible and Jesus is the Truth, revealed to us by His Holy Spirit. So in this verse, the Spirit testifies that Jesus is called God and is God.

In Colossians 2:9, the Bible says, *"For in Christ all the fullness of the Deity lives in bodily form."* How holy is Jesus if "all" of God lives in Him!

Reading the previous verse, Colossians 2:8, the Bible says as a warning, *"See to it that no one takes you captive through hollow and deceptive philosophy, which depends on human tradition and basic principles of this world rather than on Christ."*

All Satan has to do is change one word in Scripture and doubt and deception sets in. I remember hearing a person say once that his church rewrote the Bible and added an "a" to John 1:1, hoping to diminish the deity of Jesus as God. Be warned that tampering with God's Word will surely deceive you, and lead you down a path which leads to hell! We'll read more about hell later, but for now, be comforted knowing that if you have the Holy Spirit, you won't go there!

Acts 5:3-4, *"Then Peter said, 'Ananias, how is it that Satan has so filled your heart that you have lied to the Holy Spirit and have kept for yourself some of the money you received for the land? Didn't it belong to you before it was sold? And after it was sold, wasn't the money at your disposal? What made you think of doing such a thing? You have not lied to men but to God.'"*

One of my favorite stories in the Bible is when Jesus is resurrected from the dead. The Trinity of God is so clearly shown that it cannot be denied! Now we know that only God can resurrect, and we know there is perfect harmony written in God's Word. How clearly then God reveals Himself in His Word!

In 1 Thessalonians 1:10, the Bible says, *"and to wait for His Son from Heaven, whom He raised from the dead, Jesus, who rescues us from the coming wrath."*
So God the Father raised Jesus from the dead.

In Acts 3:26, the Bible says, *"When God raised up His servant, He sent Him first to you to bless you by turning each of you from your wicked ways."*
Again, God the Father said He raised Jesus from the dead.

So, the One True God raised Jesus from the dead. Now let's read on and learn what Jesus had to say about His resurrection.

In John 2:19-21, the Bible says, *"Jesus answered them, destroy this temple, and I will raise it again in three days."*

But the temple Jesus had spoken of was His body! Did you catch the full meaning of this Scripture? Jesus declared Himself God. Now we know there is only one true God, so think of God the Father and God the Son as the same person! It gets better!

Now read in Romans 8:11 where the Bible says, *"And if the Spirit of Him who raised Jesus from the dead is living in you, He who raised Christ from the dead will also give life to your mortal bodies through His Spirit, who lives in you."*

Here, the Holy Spirit reveals that He raised Jesus from the dead! And so it is, the Trinity has presented Himself as three persons, being the one and only True God, of whom there is no other like Him!

Now, you can understand John 10:25-30 where the Bible says, *"Jesus answered, 'I did tell you, but you do not believe. The miracles I do in My Father's name speak for Me, but you do not believe because you are not My sheep. My sheep listen to My voice; I know them and they follow Me. I, Jesus, give them eternal life, and they shall never perish; no one can snatch them out of My hand. My Father, who has given them to Me, is greater than all, but no one can snatch them out of My Father's hand. I, Jesus, and the Father are one!'"*

Put your faith and trust in God only; but know who God is, or you will not understand even the simple teachings that make us to be born again followers of Jesus Christ. God's grace comes to us, and when we place our trust in God, it is that believing faith that assures us of all the promises of God to come. God's will; God's way; God's timing for God's glory! Amen to THAT! Now that you have a clear picture of who God is, and how God has revealed Himself to the world, we should spend a little more time on the attributes of God. Since we agree that there is no other like Him. We should know what these unique qualities are.

I'll list some, but since our God is perfect, the list would be much greater! We've already looked at one of His attributes: the Trinity. Only our Creator God can be alive in heaven and on earth at the same time. While God the Father is on His throne, His son Jesus, sits to His right, and His Holy Spirit is at work in the world and in the hearts of His church, to complete the works of His will for His glory!

Another attribute is righteousness. He alone is righteous. All of mankind have sinned and fall short of the righteousness of God.

In Psalms 116:5, the Bible says, *"The Lord is gracious and righteous; our God is full of compassion."*

In 1 John 1:9, the Bible says, *"If we confess our sins, He is faithful and just and will forgive us our sins and purify us from all unrighteousness."*

When God forgives, we become righteous in His eyes. We'll discuss more about the Lamb of God, Jesus, and the blood of Jesus covering our sins later.

Another attribute of God is that He is <u>sovereign</u>. God is in complete control. God knows what He is doing, and He knows what is best for us. He chose to give us free will choices, and He disciplines those He loves. I personally don't call our will "free", but I acknowledge God's provision to give us the ability to choose as a freedom of choice. If I choose well, I find myself in God's will for that moment. If I choose poorly, I subject myself to God's discipline. Adam and Eve's choices resulted in sin, and we can't blame that on a sovereign God.

> I think if you can understand what is being said in John 7:17, *"If anyone chooses to do God's will, he will find out whether or not my teaching comes from God or whether I speak on my own."*

By faith, I believe God is sovereign and when free will and choice confuse me, I assume my understanding is incomplete, and I move on. My faith, then, is in Jesus and what He has done; and not what I, His creation, understand.

Another attribute of God is that He is <u>holy</u>. God is perfect. God is divine. Totally without faults. The Bible is filled with Scripture declaring that God is holy, and many describe His holiness.

> My favorite verse on His holiness is in Isaiah 6:3, *"Holy, Holy, Holy is the Lord Almighty; the whole earth is full of His glory."*

Holy is God the Father; Holy is God the Son; Holy is the Spirit of God!

Another attribute of God is that He is <u>merciful</u>. God does not give us what we deserve for our choices of sin, which would be death. Instead, because of His mercy, God offers us a way to salvation. When you understand the awesomeness of His mercy, you will appreciate what He has done on the cross for us.

Another attribute of God is that He is <u>love</u>. The key to understanding this attribute is to understand that God doesn't just have love to give, or loves us deeply, but that He is love! Get your Bible out and read 1 John 4, starting at verse 7 and read until verse 21.

> 1 John 4:16 says, *"...God is love. Whoever lives in love, lives in God, and God in him."*

This verse is referring to God the Holy Spirit in you. Remember, God the Father is in heaven sitting on His throne and Jesus is sitting by His right hand and His Spirit is living in those who believe and receive Him. And so because you have the Spirit, you have the Son, Jesus, and you have the Father, because they are one!

There are many other attributes of God, but we've discussed enough of them to give you a clear picture of who the Triune God of creation is, and how they work together to equip us to do His will. For example: God is omniscient; He knows everything and His knowledge is complete. God is omnipotent; He is all powerful, and He can do all things that He chooses to do. Since He is perfect, He would never consider doing anything against His nature. God is omnipresent; He is present in all places at all times. God sees all things: past, present and future. God is also immutable; He is unchanging. He is the same today as He was yesterday and will be the same tomorrow.

Now that you have a better picture of who God is, we can have fun learning more about Him and the ways He reveals Himself to us. Only by reading God's Word can a person come to know God in a personal way. If you listen only to sermons or teachers, you will only learn what they believe about God. What matters most is that you give God opportunities to reveal truth to you. It is a good thing to know God and all you can gather from reading, hearing, and understanding His word. Then, do what it says! We call that obedience. And as important it is to know God and to do His will, it is more important that God comes to know you personally!

To bring this chapter to a close, let me encourage you to take the things you learn about God and prove them to be true by finding supporting Scripture that say the same thing. I'll give a couple of examples, then move on.

We just discussed that God is omnipresent: that is, He is everywhere at the same time and all the time. To grow in your understanding of the Trinity of God, look for verses that refer to God, either Father, Son, or Spirit.

> In 1 Kings 8:27, the Bible says, *"But will God really dwell on earth? The heavens, even the highest heaven, cannot contain You. How much less this temple I have built."*

Here, Solomon prays and talks to God the Father about the greatness of God. This Old Testament story reveals how God chooses to indwell the temple that has been built for Him.

> In Matthew 28:18-20, the Bible says, *"Then Jesus came to them and said, 'All authority in heaven and on earth has been given to me. Therefore, go and make disciples of all nations, baptizing them in the name of the Father, and of the Son, and of the Holy Spirit, and teaching*

them to obey everything I have commanded you. And surely I am with you always, to the very end of the age.'"

The above verse refers to the second person of the Trinity, the Son; Jesus; and declares He will be with you always, even to the end of time. Only God is everywhere at the same time, all the time. This verse supports what God revealed in 1 Kings 8:27 to Solomon, and is still true today. Did you catch that we, believers, baptize new disciples in the name of the Father, and of the Son, and of the Holy Spirit? They are one God.

> Add to this Psalm 139:7-10, where the Bible says, *"Where can I go from your Spirit? Where can I flee from your presence? If I go up to the heavens, you are there. If I rise on the wings of the dawn, if I settle on the far side of the sea, even there Your hand will guide me, Your right hand will hold me fast."*

This verse refers to the third person of God, the Holy Spirit. Again, omnipresent. Again, only God is everywhere, always, at the same time! This verse confirms what is revealed in 1 Kings 8:27 and Matthew 28:20. The Holy Spirit is God; He's alive; He's in all believers; and if you have the Spirit, you have Jesus, and you have the Father, because they are one!

We also just discussed that God is omniscient. God knows everything and His knowledge is complete. So let's go looking for the Trinity in omniscience, which only God has this truth.

> In 1 John 3:20, the Bible says, *"For God is greater than our hearts, and He knows everything."* So God the Father knows everything.

> In John 16: 29-30, the Bible says, *"Then Jesus' disciples said, 'Now You are speaking clearly and without figures of speech. Now we can see that You know all things and that You do not even need to have anyone ask You questions. This makes us believe that You came from God.'"*

Only God knows "all things". Only God knows what we are thinking, even before we think it! God the Father was on His throne in heaven when Jesus was speaking to His disciples. Jesus only taught what He saw the Father teach, thus, as it was in John 1:1, Jesus was with God, and Jesus has always been God.

> In 1 Corinthians 2:10-11, the Bible says, *"But God has revealed it to us by His Spirit. The Spirit searches all things, even the deep things of God. For who among men knows the thoughts of a man except the man's*

spirit within him? In the same way no one knows the thoughts of God except the Spirit of God."

Another profound verse! Only God and I know my own thoughts, yet John 16:30 said Jesus knows! And this verse says the Holy Spirit knows! Who knows the thoughts of God except God himself? Remember, the Bible says there is no one like Him! If there is no one like Him, God Himself has revealed the truth about Himself using the person of His Holy Spirit! Going deeper; this is the same Spirit that born again believers receive into their hearts when they receive Him as Lord! Theologically, you receive the Holy Spirit of God. Doctrinally, sound teaching reveals that when you receive His Spirit, you receive Jesus the Christ as Lord and Savior, and you receive and know the Father as well, because they are one!

So, as you read the Bible, be thinking about how awesome and unique God is! Build your foundation on Him and Him alone, while being sure you know all of Him, not just the Father, but the Son and Holy Spirit as well! With God, all things are possible, so seek to be with Him! Pray that He comes to know you, or one day soon, He will come for His church and you will be left behind!

A SIMPLE ILLUSTRATION OF "TRINITY"

I want you to picture in your mind a bowling ball; a round object with three finger holes in it. Now picture in your mind, the ball being able to divide itself into thirds. Don't take it apart; just imagine three equal parts, but one ball.

Now, so I can illustrate my point, let's give each third a name. We'll call the whole ball God, and we'll call one-third of the ball God the Father; one-third of the ball God the Son, and one-third of the ball God the Holy Spirit. One ball, but revealed to us in our illustration as three different parts, or persons since we gave it names.

Now, the three finger holes in our image, we can picture them in the center of the part we have called God the Son.

Now, let our minds go a little farther. Let's say this ball is alive. Our ball breathes, moves, has power, has a will of its own, can communicate with us, and can talk to us! Our ball is one-of-a-kind!

Now let's picture in our minds a piece of paper. Our paper has no power. It is light and can be blown away. It can be cut, bent, wrinkled and burnt. One piece of paper is weak and fragile, but as in real life there is strength in numbers. So for the sake of our illustration, let's think of our paper as alive physically, but dead spiritually.

If God's Holy Spirit moves into our paper, the paper can be changed into a new creation and can become powerful in its own right. This new paper product can now be drawn to our ball. For now, we'll call this pile of paper our church body and we'll let the finger holes of our ball be filled with our paper.

Remember, one-third of our ball is called "God the Son". Another name for the Son of God is Jesus, so in reality in our illustration, our paper is now in Jesus and Jesus is in our paper.

Let's do a rabbit trail to expand our thoughts. Think of our paper, now alive in Christ, as His body, and Jesus is the Head. There are seven billion people alive physically on earth today. Let's assume one billion of these people have become like our paper, and are now living in Jesus. Since the world began, the number of believers in Christ could be ten billion!

Back to our illustration. We can fit these ten billion papers, or believers, into the finger holes of our ball and call them in Jesus.

Now here comes the hard part of our story. To grasp the whole picture and keep it in perspective, if ten billion papers, or people, can fit into the finger holes of our ball, the actual size of our ball must be much larger than we first imagined! It's HUMUNGEOUS!

> The Bible says in Isaiah 66 that, *"Heaven is God's throne, and the earth is God's footstool!"* It also says that God's hand made all things!

Picture the earth and God's foot can rest on it! Now look down at your own foot and see how big it is compared to the rest of your body! So the point of this illustration: the next time you picture God's foot being as large as our earth, look way up and beyond to see God's face! And if you can picture in your mind a bowling ball so large that it would block out the light of the sun from your view, you will then realize how small the finger holes of the ball are in comparison!

We, God's creation, cannot explain our Creator, God. What we can do is believe He exists. We can believe He is Spirit; He is Love; He is Just; He is Powerful; He created all things and works all things for good for all who love Him; He knows all things; He is perfect...and the list goes on and on! To know more about Him; read His word, pray, do what He tells you to do! LOVE HIM!

THE FULLNESS OF GOD

Holy, Holy, Holy; all three; the Trinity;
Three persons; Holy One; revealed so blind might see.
All knowing; all caring; all places; all the time;
Unchanging; all righteous; all sovereign; all rhyme.

Is Mercy; is Holy; is Spirit; is Love;
He wants you to love Him; He rules from above.
Your Savior; Redeemer; your Hope in distress;
Lord Jesus; our Shepherd; our way to success.

His Spirit; Our Counselor; His Seal; He's mine;
In Father; in Son; in Spirit; Divine.
My Hope; my Righteousness; my Savior; my Talk;
My Armor; my Builder; my Foundation; my Rock.

Creation declares His majesty,
And so do I, now that I'm free.
He came to seek what once was lost,
He came to die to pay the cost.

He came, praise God, to show us the way.
He's coming again for our judgement day.
He numbered your days; He knows your last breath.
You choose; eternal life or eternal death?

The cool part about writing a poem is that the author can leave it up to the reader to figure out what the poem is saying, or, the writer can share with you what he was thinking as he wrote.

About verse one, I used the attributes of God to show how God Himself has revealed Himself to us in His word, the Bible, God used His Holy Spirit to inspire several writers over several years to write several things about Himself. In this verse, the connecting word is "all". God alone is holy and all three are holy. God alone is everywhere all the time, and all three are there, acknowledging then that all three are the one true God, which is why there is no one like our Creator God! All three persons live together in perfect harmony and work together for the glory of God.

In verse two, we continue to develop our relationship with God and start to focus on Jesus. We know that God is love; not just loving us or loveable, but "is"! HE IS LOVE. If you have not yet received His love, you only know about His love! I asked God what the message should be in verse two and He said, "Is He your Lord?" So, the first word in each line declares this question. Line 1 "Is", line 2 "He", line 3 "Your", and line 4 "Lord". So as you read, you ask yourself, "Is He my Lord?" "Do I believe He is love?" "Can I picture Him as Spirit; as Holy; as Judge; as the one with sovereign power yet sender of His love and grace?" "Does He know you yet?"

In verse three, we talk about the third person of God, the Holy Spirit.

In Acts 1:7-8, the Bible says, *"Jesus said to them, 'It is not for you to know the times or dates the Father has set by His own authority. But you will receive power when the Holy Spirit comes on you; and you will be my witnesses in Jerusalem, and in all Judea and Samaria, and to the ends of the earth.'"*

In 2 Corinthians 1:21-22, the Bible says, *"Now it is God who makes both us and you stand firm. He anointed us, set His seal of ownership on us, and put His Spirit in our hearts as a deposit, guaranteeing what is to come."*

And the last line of verse 3 speaks about the armor of God.

In Ephesians 6:10, the Bible says, *"Finally be strong in the Lord and in His mighty power. Put on the full armor of God so that you can take your stand against the devil's schemes."*

This armor Paul is talking about is the belt of truth, the breastplate of righteousness, the foot protection of the gospel, the shield of faith, the helmet of salvation and the sword of the Spirit, which is the Scripture. Notice as you read, God never tells you to take this armor off! Prayer will be your connection to God, and His Spirit in you will counsel and guide you daily as you pick up your cross and walk with Him!

Our last verse. God has always been, and will always be. He is perfect in every way and we assume He is perfectly content in Himself. Think of Him as perfect love. God the Father, being Spirit; His Son, also Spirit only in eternity past; both being filled with the Holy Spirit. All three existing together as one God. The only true God.

Then, one day, they decided to speak into nothing and create more to worship and praise them and bring them more glory. And so it was! God the Father created, through His Son, the heavens and the earth and mankind began. God was in control of all things, and still is in control. He has a purpose and a plan and His will is going to prevail! He knew us before the creation story, and He knows who will receive Him as Lord, and soon He will be returning for His church, which the Bible says is made up of all believers in Christ. God the Father gave His Son, Jesus, a list with the names of all whom He chose to spend eternity with Him and Jesus has lost none!

So God knows the future, and we know He has a place in heaven for His church and He has a list to confirm our reservation or deny our entry. So, get on the list before He returns!

Read the Bible, believe what it says, do what it says, realize you are a sinner in need of a Savior. Believe that Jesus is the Lamb of God. Believe He is God. Believe He is the Word, the Truth, the Life, and the Way. Confess your sins to Him. Ask for forgiveness. Receive His free gift of salvation, receive His Spirit into your heart, then repent, follow Him, be baptized, obey His teachings and allow Him to make you into the person He wants you to be! Jesus is coming soon and your reward is with Him and your reward is eternal life with Him!

This is what God had planned from our beginning and He will receive all His glory due Him. The Bible teaches that today is your day of salvation. Choose Life, so that you may live.

THE ONE YOU NEED

I am the one you need, though it could be you don't know it.
I'm the answer to your prayers, if you ask, I'll gladly show it.

There is power in My name, though I have a humble heart.
I've been known to live and die, so that we would never part.

There is grace each place I am, where I am, My love will follow.
Yes, and with Me, there is life, I can fill you if you're hollow.

So if I caught your eye, or perhaps your full attention.
Let Me tell you who I am, and the reason this I mention.

I am Jesus, Son of God, I'm the Truth, the Life, the Way.
Yes, I am the one you need, on this special Valentine's Day!

THE TRINITY

God: Father; Lord; Maker of heaven and earth;
Whose word is life; whose word is light; whose word gave birth.
Creator; Protector; Enforcer; in control of time, space and mystery,
Eternal in every way known to man; whose prophecy precedes history.

Jesus: Son of God; Holy Child; Redeemer; Our life, light and way.
Who lived; died and rose again; ascended; returning one day.
Whose blood was shed to pay for sin; He saved us on the cross;
By grace and faith we live today; to verify His loss.

Holy Spirit: Revealer of Truth; Divine Counselor; Inspired Guide;
A force that brings life and light to humanity; identity of bride.
A godly power; offered to all who seek and obey His advice;
His living proof; given to believers who are born twice.

If you want His redemption, forgiveness and grace;
Speak humbly to Jesus; repent to His face
Be honest and caring and ask for His light;
Be saved; His holy presence will make your heart right!

His Spirit; now with you, will show you the way,
His word will now guide you; be patient and pray.
Don't take life for granted; continue to grow,
Build faith now in Jesus and let His love flow!

Chapter 2
GOD'S GRACE

Grace is God's free gift to mankind, it is not deserved by us, but God in His great love for us gave and continues to bless us with it. Though sin came into humanity through Adam and Eve; God's grace came directly from Him, and it is grace by which we are saved. It is grace that gives each human time to sort out the things that God has done for us, and time also to choose or reject Christ. By extending the gift of grace to us, God is displaying His sovereignty over mankind, and despite mankind's sinful nature, God continues to build His church.

As I look back on my past days without Christ, I can see clearly God's grace covering my sinful behavior every step of the way. And yet, I also recall that I never knew grace! It was there; absolutely; but I didn't know it! I guess that's why I love and appreciate grace so much today, as I now live in His light and can humbly appreciate what Jesus saw in me back then; and merciful grace was there! As the song says: grace is amazing; and I am amazed over and over as His grace continues to work in my life as well as everywhere!

> Ephesians 2:8-9, the Bible says, *"For it is by grace you have been saved, through faith, and this not from yourselves, it is the gift of God, not by works so that no one can boast.*

This verse repeats what God revealed in 2:5 and you should read it over and over until you understand what God is saying, so you might believe it is true.

In this passage, Paul describes himself as an apostle of Christ Jesus by the will of God. An apostle because he encountered Jesus on the road to Damascus and knew Jesus was Lord. Paul is writing to the church in Ephesus; the faithful followers and believers in Jesus. Paul is reviewing for them what God had done for them.

Our relationship with God was never intended to be a religious thing, but a spiritual experience as we worship and praise Him. It is God who chose us and His grace is offered to everyone whether they know it or not! As God draws people to Himself, grace gives us time to get to know who He is and what He has accomplished on the cross. And when we come to believe in His story, we ask for forgiveness and make peace with Him and during this heartfelt moment, we become His and He seals us in Christ by placing His Holy Spirit in us.

2 Corinthians 5:17-18 says, *"Therefore, if anyone is in Christ, he is a new creation, the old sinful nature is gone, the new life has come! All this is from God, who reconciled us to Himself through Christ, and gave us the ministry of reconciliation."*

Romans 6:6 says, *"For we know that our old self was crucified with Him so that the body of sin might be done away with, that we should no longer be slaves to sin, because anyone who has died has been freed from sin."* Verse 8 says, *"Now if we died with Christ, we believe that we will also live with Him".*

Romans 8:13 says, *"For if you live according to the sinful nature, you will die; but if you live by the Spirit, you put to death the misdeeds of the body and you will live, because these who are led by the Spirit of God are sons of God."*

So there it is again, describing what God has done through His grace, through the cross, for those who believe what He has done and place their faith totally in Him; for His Glory! And to seal the deal for those He redeemed, He seals us with His Holy Spirit until the day Jesus returns with our reward: Himself! Jesus is our Lord. Jesus is our Salvation! Jesus is the Truth, the Life and the Way. Jesus is the door we must go to! Jesus is the gate we must enter! Jesus is the name in which we will be saved!

Romans 5:20 says, *"The law was added so that the trespass might increase. But where sin increased, grace increased all the more, so that just as sin reigned in death, so also grace might reign through righteousness to bring eternal life through Jesus Christ our Lord."*

Remember the story of how sin entered the world through the sin of Adam? Well, through Jesus, the penalty of sin, which is death, was paid for and righteousness is obtainable through Christ. So grace is God's gift to you; receive the gift and start pleasing God!

1 John 2:15 says, *"Do not love the world or anything in the world. If anyone loves the world, the love of the Father is not in him."*

This was written to believers as a warning, but is good advice to those who are spiritually dead also!

A TESTIMONY ABOUT GOD'S GRACE

In December of 1949, a baby was born into this world and this baby's parents named the child John Roger Drews. They chose the first name John after my Mom's grandpa, John Gustafson; my Dad's name was Roger Drews, which I inherited both. In December of 2014, my Mom gave me two books. One was Grandpa John's catechism book written in Swedish, dated 1876. The other book, dated 1882, was signed by Grandpa John and was a bi-lingual book he read as he prepared to learn English when he left Sweden to come to America. My point is this: as a child, I knew nothing about anything! And it took 65 years of my life to hear details of the life of my great Grandpa! Yes, better late than never, but my second point is this: I didn't know because I didn't ask! As I have now pondered how many other questions did I never ask, I realized there would be no reason to share about God's grace in my life, since most of my life I didn't even know what God's grace was! So, here's the idea I had, and will now explain. Instead of telling my life's story from my past perspective; I will tell it from today's perspective, which happens to be February 4th, 2015. So let's start over!

I was born into the world in 1949 and I have a birth certificate to prove the event. Let me share what the Bible says about us babies:

> Psalm 139:13-16 says, "For You, God, created my inmost being; You knit me together in my mother's womb. I praise You because I am fearfully and wonderfully made; Your works are wonderful, I know that full well. My frame was not hidden from You when I was made in the secret place. When I was woven together in the depths of the earth, Your eyes saw my unformed body. All the days ordained for me were written in Your book before one of them came to be."

> In Luke 12:7 Jesus says, "Indeed, the very hairs of your head are all numbered by God."

Like so many children these days, we grew up hearing stories from our parents about "why they decided to have me" or "when they decided to have another child" or "how they planned to have three kids and the fourth was an accident". But here is the truth! God is in control. He chose when I would be conceived and when I would be born and even what I would look like. He knew great details about me, which included the number of hairs on my head! And then the hard to comprehend fact of when I would die! So my first understanding of the application of grace in my life was when my parents took credit for my birth, though ownership was God's and my parents were my care givers. My point and God's point is this: We all have earthly parents who name us, raise us, and teach us things, but the true source of all things is God! My parents should have read the Bible, adjusted their lives to His will, and raised their children in a way that reflects Jesus! In this story, my parents were busy raising five children and pursuing their understanding of life, liberty and the pursuit of happiness. The spiritual life was never a factor, which left us all dead in our sins, which caused some radical behavior, to say the least! On a positive note, I did love my parents and felt loved most of the time. I think they did the best they could with the circumstances they lived in. And my Mom is still living, 86, and doing well and my love and appreciation for her grows each year as my understanding of God's Word increases and my understanding of the verse that says "Honor your father and mother" becomes more complete.

Moving forward three weeks, my next big event was church baptism. I don't recall the details, but my parents said I was sprinkled with water in believers baptism which was customary in the Saint John's Lutheran Church in Mound, Minnesota and my parents were given a baptism certificate, stamped, witnessed and signed as proof of my salvation. My Mom kept this document for years and in 1992 she gave it to me and I still have it, now in my drawer!

Evangelical churches would call this event a "baby dedication". They would say my parents were dedicating their son to God and that they were declaring to God and the congregation that, in this case, John, would be raised in a Christian home, and that they would see to it that I would read and understand the Bible, and that I would be encouraged to live my life in a way pleasing to the Lord.

To this event I say this; before a person can be saved, you must come to the understanding that you are lost! God's grace will cover these children until the age of accountability arrives. When it arrives, and I am made aware that I am a sinner, I must then come to believe that God exists; that He has a purpose and a plan for my life; that my sin separates me from God; that the reward or wages for sin is death; and that Jesus is the Lamb of God; who died on the cross to pay the penalty of all sin; who died for me so that I might live with Him in heaven for eternity. Believing these things, I am ready to repent. I ask for forgiveness; I receive His forgiveness; He comes into my heart and seals me with His Holy Spirit; and being bought with a price, I now belong to Him and soon He will return to gather all those who have been born again and are now living in Christ.

So, looking back on that day, I think the date of my salvation was premature, but as grace would have it, in November of 1996, I did come to the saving knowledge of the cross; I did become a born again follower of Jesus Christ; I am in Christ and He is in me and I have a personal love relationship with Jesus Christ. I know Him and He knows me, and I confidently look forward to heaven where I will receive my eternal body and live with Him forever.

I wonder sometimes if I would have lived my life differently if I hadn't believed I was okay with God because I was baptized? I had no reason to believe there wasn't a

God or a hell! I do love grace and learned a lesson worthy of mention: No matter how sincere your beliefs are, if truth reveals your beliefs to be wrong, they are truly and sincerely wrong!

There was another event in my childhood that I clearly remember that influenced my life and the life of my parents. I was 12, in seventh grade and I could get out of school 3 hours early on Wednesdays if I went to a Saint John's Lutheran Church confirmation class. I went, but I don't remember how many times. But I do remember graduating, getting a certificate of confirmation and what Pastor Sadness said to our parents. He said, and I quote, "This has been a disappointing year for me and this class of 30 students is the worst I've ever had. Undisciplined, unprepared and uninterested in learning!"

Two things came from his declaration of disappointment. One, my parents were offended and to the best of my knowledge, never went back to church! Secondly, I never went back there either until 1997, shortly after becoming a Christian. I visited again twice in December of 2014 as they did my brother Scott's funeral there and I really liked their current pastor; a sincere man of compassion and a beautiful voice.

Pastor Sadness could have spoken in a more loving way, but to his credit, we were a bunch of rebellious youth! While visiting, I saw a picture of our class and was reminded of who all was in our class! We were a rowdy bunch and got a little worse as we reached our teens, twenty, thirties, etc. Again my point is this: my confirmation confirmed one thing: I was a sinner who didn't know God, Jesus or the Holy Spirit! I was lost and didn't care and I lived my life another thirty-five years proving it! Again, grace was there, increasing when needed, until God drew me to Himself!

Okay, back to the history of my childhood! I enjoyed my youth as far back as I can remember. I played a lot of baseball, from t-ball to Little League to Babe Ruth League to high school. I grew up in a neighborhood with a lot of kids and most of us played ball daily at our neighborhood parks from spring to fall; it never got old! I lived on Lake Minnetonka and fished from our dock a lot, plus swam daily all summer. I remember playing "Cowboys and Indians" often. I climbed trees often, built forts, and took walks to Grimm's store for ice cream cones most days in the summer. In my younger years, I got to spend time at my grandparents, a town 150 miles away, usually a month at a time. All great memories and fun days! And as far as school goes: I went but nothing caught my attention much and I got by. Because my Dad enjoyed the outdoors as much as working, I spent many hours hunting deer, ducks, partridge, pheasant, and to be honest, anything that was in the woods or back yard! We canoed a lot and caught a lot of fish! We golfed a lot, camped out quite often and watched sports on the TV on weekends. Life was good! I could recall some anger, foul language, my Dad's belt and a few fights, but I choose not to remember those unhappy moments!

Then came the teenage years! Looking back, we can call these years covered by God's grace; totally! At 13, my first motorcycle: a 90cc Yamaha. Daily accidents as I learned to pop wheelies while navigating our back yard. Permits were available at 14 for 50cc bikes. My first road accident came before I had my driver's license! At 14, I started noticing girls and their pretty faces. At 15, I noticed girls had more than pretty faces! At 17, I graduated from high school. At 18, I got married. At 19, I graduated from Dunwoody Trade School's electrical department and joined the local 292 Union.

At this point in time, life was good. I'm looking back at God's grace during this time period and don't want to spend time telling about sin issues of my past teenage years. There were moments, like my first kiss, my first sexual fornication, my first drink, my first of several driving tickets, my first snowmobile accident, my first boat accident and those kind of things, but some stories should be put to rest and most of my teenage stories fall into that category!

At 21, I finished my electrical apprenticeship and passed my Class A Journeyman's test and received my license. I bought my first house; I bought my first corvette, I bought my first new boat and saw my daughter Shelley be born. Correction; I was there when she was born! I don't do well looking at blood! And then the bad news; I legally walked into a bar and had my first drink! More bad news: I liked it!

To save time, I'll summarize my life from 22 to 42! I continued pursuing my love for sports. I played on 2 softball teams while coaching Little League baseball with my son, Greg. I played volleyball on a regular basis and enjoyed it greatly. I spent lots of time hunting, fishing and camping. I bowled on leagues and traveled to various countries often. I went on to own Drews Electric; Drews Trenching; Sunlight Tanning Salon and Gym of Mound; Healthy Tan in Grand Rapids and finally Drews Sports Cards; selling baseball and all other sports cards and collectables. Made money; spent money; these parts of my life were good!

Unfortunately, there was another side of me I haven't yet mentioned! I did all the above things under the influence of drugs, alcohol, pride and arrogance. There were several bar fights, adultery, two divorces, fornication, family neglect and other behavior too shameful to discuss.

Looking back, I can see the harm that came from my behavior, and if I could, I would change most of my choices that I made. But, also looking back, I enjoyed most of my days! I worked hard for my money and enjoyed spending it! I knew I was radical in my behavior, but I liked it most of the time! I was okay with my pride; my self-centeredness; and my successes and failures. Physically, I stayed in shape and was strong. Socially, I felt I was becoming a better person as I got older. Mentally, well, I've always been a little different! Spiritually, I was baptized and confirmed, so I figured I'd deal with God later, someday, or after I died.

Looking back, I know now exactly where I was. Total darkness. Totally comfortable in my sin and my sinful nature. Ignorant of the Bible and what stories God reveals in it and ignorant of whom Jesus was and is. I was LOST! Sincerely lost and sincerely wrong!

Now, what I used to call the better years: from 43-46. I had made peace with my Dad over our past dealings and visited my Mom and Dad whenever I went home to Mound. I was living in Grand Rapids, Minnesota, which I liked a lot. I opened a new card shop in a new location of town, but same name: Drews Sports Cards. Being self-employed, I made a good cash income, yet could fish or play whenever I chose. My hours were flexible during weekdays, but many times I'd open nights and weekends when the weather was bad. I dated some, but no commitments. My daughter, Shelley, lived out of town and then out of state, but she visited Grand Rapids and we went on a cool vacation together in Mexico. My son, Greg, lived in Vegas and said he was doing well, so I was happy for him. My Dad, brothers and sisters came to town fairly often and we enjoyed fishing, food and some bar scenes, but somewhat under control! My best friends, Will and Joyce, lived nearby and we continued to fish, bowl, volleyball and enjoyed our local food and drink places. All in all, the best years of my life up to this point; and looking back, God's grace was there!

Then came the summer of 1996. A truck driver came to my card shop and asked me if I was a Christian. My response: I went to church when I was young; got baptized, got confirmed and moved on. He shared a few verses to which I had no answer. I finally told him to come back in three months and we'd have this conversation again. I told him I would buy a Bible and read it, and when he returned, if he had lied to me in anyway, he would be using the front window to exit my shop the next time we met. Grace was definitely there! To this day, I can still see his sincere face as he shared his faith and the grin he wore even though I had just threatened him!

So, I bought a Bible: King James Version. I couldn't understand much and didn't like the language. Went back and bought a Strong's Concordance and read it. I know how to use it today, but back then: stupid! I then went back to the book store and bought a second Bible, Revised King James. I read it cover to cover, but still didn't understand much. I didn't know how to pray, so I simply said, "God, I want to know the truth, Amen". Using the second Bible as a helper, I read the first Bible from Genesis to Job.

I didn't know it yet, but God had already convinced me that He was real, and that He sent Jesus to the cross as His sacrifice to pay the price for my sins for me. I began to see that the whole Bible must be true, which meant my life had no truth in it! As I read in Job, I realized what He had suffered personally, yet held on to his faith in God, and in the end, God blessed him extremely well.

I stopped reading, thought through what I had learned, went to my bedroom and began to talk to God as if He was real. I called Him Lord, which surprised me! I realized my sins were many and I needed His forgiveness. I believed Jesus was what I was missing and I asked Him to change me. I lay down, cried a bit, and then fell asleep.

I don't remember the exact day, but it was a week day. I had overslept and I was two hours late to open my card shop. I jumped up, took a shower, and looked out the window to see what the weather looked like. And I was overwhelmed!

I had lived 46 years in black and white and as I looked out the window, everything was in color! I saw birds that I'd never paid attention to before, I saw flowers, I saw blue sky, I saw clouds, and I saw people walking towards the park. I was amazed! I had a peace that I couldn't describe! I felt loved, then I figured I must have had some sort of mental breakdown!

By now it's about noon! I walked downstairs to my card shop. I was relieved to see that no one had come to the shop yet; it didn't matter that I was so late! I began reading in the book of Matthew and was shocked again! As I read, I understood all that I was reading as if God had answered my prayer of knowing the truth!

My first customer that day turned out to be a believer himself and when I told him how weird my morning had been, he smiled and said, "You got saved last night!" We talked a while and he explained to me what had taken place. I cried tears of joy that day and every day for the next month!

So, that was my beginning point as a born again follower of Jesus Christ. During my first six months as a believer I connected with a church and made many new friends; I read four other versions of the Bible and went on my first mission trip. In January of 1998, I shut down my card shop, bought a new truck and moved to Libby, Montana to attend a missionary school called International Messengers. After graduation, I married Bonnie; went on a mission trip to Poland; started a youth center; joined a church; bought a house; went back to work for 13 years; retired; and started on Social Security. Now I am preparing for a mission trip to Guatemala with Bonnie, organized through a church in Spokane, Washington.

I've shortened the last 19 years because if I tried to share details of all the things God has changed in my life, one book wouldn't be enough! His grace is worthy of praise! And if it be God's will, I'll continue to be used by God over and over until He returns for me; one way or another!

And yes, at 65, I'm still living strong for the Lord, and He isn't done with me yet! In each season I do ministry as needed. Then, I enjoy each day as given the opportunity.

I still fish, but not too often. I golf when the weather is nice. I camp whenever we get good weather and a three day weekend. I enjoy landscaping and I find my own rocks and driftwood when I have time. I travel some; Minnesota each summer; a cruise a while back and a trip to Jamaica before that; but prefer mission trips. Went to Guatemala in 2009 and 2012, and now will go in 2016. And then, who knows! I know this, grace will be there!

GOD'S GRACE

God knew before He spoke creation,
That we would be a sinful nation.
Yet even so, as time began,
He offered grace; a gift to man.

When sin grew great; His grace was stronger.
When patience was short; His grace waited longer.
When our faith was little; He gifted us more.
When we finally humbled; He opened His door.

God chose us and sealed us and helped us believe,
His free gift; Salvation; no reason to grieve.
Position established, His Spirit now placed,
Move forward and follow, there's no time to waste.

With Jesus inside us, we trust and obey,
His grace will go with us, to face every day.
We didn't deserve Him, yet He died in our place,
Not only believers, but the whole human race.

So choose or reject Him; He died for all sin,
Decide while still able; by grace you may win.
But Spirit rejected; will guarantee death,
The offer; still pending; till you take your last breath.

For those who choose to believe in Jesus as Lord will have eternal life. All others have chosen death by default. Of your own free will you accept God's gift or not, but there will be cost, sooner or later. Keep in mind that no one is promised tomorrow, so today is a good day to make peace with God.

Jesus said He will be back and when He comes, there will be good news and bad news, depending on where you are at in your relationship with God. The good news is that all people who have been born again with His Spirit will be caught up to be with Him forever. The bad news is that soon after the believers are gone, judgment will soon follow. As the world tries to fix itself and peace seems close, seven years of tribulation happens instead! And then; heaven or hell, depending on who you choose to believe in; Jesus or Satan.

Then eternity! Time is up and over! Only eternal life or eternal death. Either way, you will get what you asked for! God knows all things and He will balance His perfect Love with His perfect justice and judge perfectly! What's in your heart?

GRACE TO JOIN HIM

The Lord will harvest His spirits, from the hearts of the believer,
And woe to the many who fall short with the deceiver.
Our Father, in control, returns to bring glory,
Replacing our faith, with His unending story.

By grace, we were given a chance to survive,
Once dead in the world; we now are alive!
The deceiver is real, but he cannot create,
Please change your desires, before it's too late!

We all came from darkness, through Jesus; our Light,
From weakness, to glory; from sorrow to delight.
Our passion is growing; our strength is desire,
The work is now flowing; our hearts are on fire!

But something is missing! Some souls still to save!
If we don't try to reach them, we allow them their grave!
So join in God's mission, which we now prepare,
If you desire God's glory, then you must show you care!

Not all can be leaving, at least not in flesh,
But prayer is important; prayer keeps our hearts fresh.
The day is soon coming, when judgment will reign,
The forgiven are taken, and the "self" ones remain.

JESUS IS YOUR FRIEND

Time goes by, in waves of emotion,
Sometimes mean nothing; some deep devotion.
In time, all things, begin and end,
Time, well spent, is with a friend.

A friend is there, when times get tough,
The times you share, are never enough.
With self, life is lonely; with friends, life is grand,
Alone, no one listens; together, all understand.

To understand, is to care about life,
Learn to forgive and you live without strife.
When you're born you start dying, there is no guarantee,
If your eyes have been blinded, seek Him who sets free.

There is truth in His freedom; He creates out of love,
It's His time that you live in; He's your friend from above.
You will hear, if you listen; take time and you will see,
What a great celebration, when His time comes for thee!

JESUS IS COMING SOON

I seek only wisdom; I need no great dreams,
For only illusion, is not what it seems.
My strength is in Jesus, and truth that He teaches,
Eternity is waiting, for the souls that He reaches.

God promised salvation; when saved, we are one,
Yes, one with the Father and one with the Son.
His Spirit is holy; He lives in our heart,
For when we accept Him; we have a new start.

His blood washed our ugly; the price was His death,
Yet through resurrection; we know He has breath.
And by His ascension, He has shown us the way,
He will be returning; our hope is today!

GET CAUGHT UP IN LIFE

Life is eternal, if you have accepted His gift,
Saved souls live forever; it is wise not to drift.
But life has no meaning, if you've not heard His call,
If you hold out with Satan; when the end comes, you fall.

Be prepared for His coming; it is time to repent,
You must turn from your sinning; hear the message He sent.
Let your eyes beam with glory; may you glow in His light,
Let your heart turn to holy; may your robe wash to white.

Make Jesus your first love, put all others behind.
If a mirror watched you living, are you seen being kind?
Are the angels rejoicing when you testimony is read?
Do you live in obedience when you take wine and bread?

I believe we surrender, just before we receive,
I believe He is faithful; He would never deceive.
So put faith in Jesus; He soon comes for His bride,
In a blink, we will meet Him; we; with Spirit inside.

LEARNING ABOUT JESUS

So many times; how hard I've tried,
To share the love, I've found inside.
But life is good, so man won't listen,
I wish they knew, the love they are missin'.

I know God's son; I've accepted His grace,
I know His plan, to save our race.
But Satan lives and uses his power,
His only end; to lame and devour.

I've been attacked and tempted of sin,
But Satan knows; with Jesus, I win.
For revelation warns of things we will see,
The signs will show us, when they will be.

Jesus is coming; I know it is soon,
And when He does, you'll sing a new tune.
So hear me now; the time is at hand,
Man's moment of truth; you'd best understand!

Chapter 3
THE FRUIT OF THE SPIRIT

Before we talk about the fruits of the Holy Spirit in our lives, I must mention that you must receive the Spirit before you can expect good fruit from your life. The Bible teaches that a good tree produces good fruit, and a bad tree produces bad fruit. Then also, a good tree cannot produce bad fruit. Simply said, a true Christian is a good tree, and will bear good works, habits, and everyday lives that reflect the love of Jesus. Then also, the true born again Christian will not be self-centered, but will be God-centered. He will try not to sin, but if he does, he confesses, repents, receives forgiveness, and quickly restores his relationship with God. The true Christian does not choose to sin, and when caught in sin, he does not stay there. If this person stays there in disobedience to God's Word, discipline will come! If discipline doesn't come, you are under God's grace OR have never truly believed in Jesus Christ as Lord. Let the following verses speak to your heart, so you may know for sure who your Master is today.

> Matthew 7:15-20, Jesus says, *"Watch out for false prophets. They come to you in sheep's clothing, but inwardly they are ferocious wolves. By their fruit you will recognize them. Do people pick grapes from thorn bushes, or figs from thistles? Likewise, every good tree bears good fruit, but a bad tree bears bad fruit. A good tree cannot bear bad fruit, and a bad tree cannot bear good fruit. Every tree that does not bear good fruit is cut down and thrown into the fire. Thus, by their fruit you will recognize them."*

People who ignore God and choose to remain in their sinful nature are easy to identify. They indulge in immoral acts of sexual pleasure, sometimes adultery, sometimes live together outside of God's provision of marriage. They have varying measures of greed, pride, boastfulness, lust, anger, selfish ambition, drunkenness, cheating, lying, and can steal without remorse.

People who come to believe in Jesus receive His Spirit, and they no longer are a slave to sin. They, out of love and obedience to God's Word, choose to do what is right in God's eyes. As a result of living for God, the Spirit in them produces visible qualities on the outside pleasing to God. Thus, our lives as believers reflect the qualities of Jesus as He works in us to produce His harvest.

LOVE

1 Timothy 6:15 says, *"God, the blessed and only Ruler, the King of kings, and Lord of lords, who alone is immortal and who lives in unapproachable light, whom no one has seen or can see."*

God lives in heaven. Our Triune God; our Father; our Savior; and His Holy Spirit. One day His chosen will be given immortal bodies and will see Him face to face. That day has not yet come.

Evil spirits are not allowed to enter the Holy, perfect place called heaven. Even our eternal soul will not be allowed there until we are born again, and then, when our time has come, we will receive our glorified bodies.

God can come to us, angels can be sent to protect us, but we don't go to visit Him. Voices come, visions come, tongues come, and other hard-to-explain things come, but never His "unapproachable light."

We love God with all our heart, soul, mind and strength. Be careful not to add an 's' on the end in an attempt to describe the truth. We have one heart, one soul, one mind. When His Spirit enters, we become His temple. We then have a heart for God, our soul is saved, our mind is being transformed, and He becomes our strength.

Galatians 5:22-23 says *"But the fruit of the Spirit is love, joy, peace, patience, kindness, goodness, faithfulness, gentleness, and self control."*

We could write a library of books just on love and still have more to say. God is love, and God shares His love with believers through His Holy Spirit. So my first comment is this: unless you receive Jesus as Lord and receive His Spirit, you have never received His love into your life. You may have seen His love, or heard about His love, but never been changed by His love. Your worldly love is learned or caught from others. You learned to "act your age" or "act like you care" or "act right", but all you became was a good actor, and never really understood what love was until love came to you through Jesus. So let's find out what God's love in you looks like.

1 Corinthians 13:4-8 says, *"Love is patient, love is kind. It does not envy, it does not boast, it is not proud. Love is not rude, it is not self-seeking, it is not easily angered, it keeps no record of wrongs. Love does not delight in evil but rejoices with the truth. It always protects, always trusts, always hopes, always perseveres, love never fails."*

Galatians 2:20 says, *"I have been crucified with Christ and I no longer live, but Christ lives in me. The life I live in the body, I live by faith in the Son of God, who loved me and gave Himself for me."*

Because Jesus lives in me, I have a close love relationship with Him. I have His Spirit, which is truth. I have power within me to overcome the world, and I can do things and receive things in His name. I know God the Father because I know Jesus and have allowed His Spirit to teach me His ways. Because I have His love, I can truly love others. I can find all my needs in Him. I can trust Him because He loves me.

John 14:15 says, *"If you love Me, you will obey what I command. And I will ask the Father, and He will give you another Counselor to be with you forever."*

1 John 2:5 says, *"But if anyone obeys His word, God's love is truly made complete in Him. This is how we know we are in Him."*

Obedience. This is what Jesus showed us during His life on earth, and this is what He commands us to do in His Word. "Thou shall," when God is speaking, is a command. Not good advice or a suggestion! If you do not obey Him, you do not love Him, and soon you will reveal the true condition of your heart.

Remember, James 1:22, *"Do not merely listen to the word, and so deceive yourself. Do what it says!"*

Many in today's world say they love, but in reality, they don't even know Him! God is love; God is alive; and if He is alive in you, prove it by the way you live! Be loveable; be loving; be lovers of righteousness. The Bible says perfect love drives out fear. God's love drives our fears away and brings hope to those who believe in Him. Do not say you love God if your actions prove you do not! Love is slow to anger. Love does what is right. We live in the world, but we give ourselves to God. If your brothers in Christ accused you of not loving God, is there enough truthful evidence to prove them wrong? If not, your reasons for your actions will not excuse you from judgment!

JOY

Just as love does, true joy comes from knowing Jesus as Lord. As the Spirit works in you, joy is there. In your heart, in your mind, in your soul, on your face, on your lips, as you sing, as you minister to others, as you face your trials, tests, and temptations. Has God made you glad? Do you have a smile on your face? If you are glad and smiling, I'm joyful!

> Hebrews 12:2 says, *"Let us fix our eyes on Jesus, the author and perfecter of our faith, who for the joy set before Him endured the cross, scorning its shame, and sat down at the right hand of the throne of God."*

Jesus had joy in His sufferings, because He knew He was dying for the sins of the world. His death paid for the penalty of our sins! We can now choose to live with Him because He died in our place. Jesus was the perfect sacrifice; the Lamb of God. And His obedience was joyful to Him! Is your obedience; your love; joyful to you? It should be!

> James 1:2 says, *"Consider it pure joy, my brothers, whenever you face trials of many kinds, because you know that the testing of your faith produces perseverance."*

"My brothers" means "fellow believers". "Many kinds of trials" means they are coming, they might offend you, and God is testing you so you may know how strong your faith is. Satan and his followers tempt your faith in hopes of pulling you into sin, where he wants you. Testing is given by God to draw you closer to Him and away from sin.

PEACE

Not everyone has peace in their lives, but true Christians do. It's a fruit that comes from the Spirit within you. The world may war against your body and cause you physical pain, but inside you, where the Spirit is working and giving you inner peace and strength to endure; there is your hope and inspiration to carry on.

> In Matthew 10:34-36, Jesus says, *"Do not suppose that I have come to bring peace to the earth. I did not come to bring peace, but a sword. For I have come to turn a man against his father, a daughter against her mother, a daughter-in-law against her mother-in-law; a man's enemies will be the members of his own household."*

> Jesus said to His followers in John 16:33 *"I have told you these things, so that in Me you may have peace. In this world you will have trouble. But take heart! I have overcome the world."*

Together these verses show the peace the world will not have, contrasted by the peace believers will have. God comes first; always! If a father loves God and chooses to follow Jesus and his son does not, there is no peace between them. What does darkness and light have in common? Jesus says "nothing". What then do people who live in sin have in common with those who are slaves to righteousness? Jesus says "nothing". True peace comes from God to those who remain "in Him". In His will. In His Word. Choosing to do His plans, in His way, for God's glory.

> Romans 8:6 says, *"The mind of sinful man is death, but the mind controlled by the Spirit is life and peace."*

If you are a born again follower of Jesus Christ, you have the truth in you, and you have life in you, and you have the way that leads to eternal life, and you have spiritual peace, which allows you to overcome the world just as Jesus did.

> Isaiah 32:17 says, *"The fruit of righteousness will be peace, the effect of righteousness will be quietness and confidence forever."*

True Christians have been given His righteousness, and therefore have or will have peace. Also, the Spirit led man has a righteous attitude despite the trouble around him attacking his flesh.

PATIENCE

Just as God is love, the Bible says God is patient. We remember the flood that God sent that killed all the living except one family and a bunch of animals, and we remember Jesus when he went into a place of worship and angrily turned over tables and sent people out of there. So we know this: there is a difference between righteous anger and sinful anger. Since God is righteous, His anger is also just. His followers are slaves to righteousness, so they are expected to do what is right, not in our power and strength, but His. His Spirit working in us will produce patience, and the world will see the outward affects of our inward changes. If you say you have no patience, you are saying you have no love, which means you have no desire to obey God, which means you obey Satan, and he is then your lord. So I remind you of this statement that I use from time to time; "What you know in your head is what you talk about, but what you believe in your heart to be true is what you do in your daily life." Don't simply read the Bible, and in doing so, deceive yourself; do what it says! What you believe is how you live, and others see how you live. Don't let your actions cause others to stumble.

> Proverbs 19:11 says, *"A man's wisdom gives him patience; it is to his glory to overlook an offence."*

> Colossians 3:12 says, *"Therefore, as God's chosen people, holy and dearly loved, clothe yourselves with compassion, kindness, humility, gentleness, and patience."*

As Christians, we should strive to do what is right every day, day by day. We should always have a forgiving attitude just as Christ did. We should follow Christ's examples in all things, and with Him, this is possible. Our hearts should have peace and joy in them, and we should be thankful that we do. We should always be learning from His word, knowing the world is always watching and we are His representative.

When you pray in Jesus' name, say this, "Whatever it takes Lord, give me more patience! Amen." Now, wait on His answer, it will come. Warning! The answer may test your faith, but if you persevere, you will receive more patience!

KINDNESS

Everyone knows we should be kind; to people, ourselves, strangers, and animals, etc. But most people are rude, in a hurry, self-centered, angry at times, and victims of other people's unkindness, so we become bitter and uncaring. Then enters the Spirit at work in our hearts, and we become aware of God's love and how He wants us to live for Him for His glory. So we become kinder.

> Proverbs 12:25, *"An anxious heart weighs a man down, but a kind word cheers him up."*

> Philippians 4:6 says, *"Do not be anxious about anything, but in everything, by prayer and petition, with thanksgiving, present your requests to God."*

Be a peacemaker, an encourager, and pray for those in need, so they may know your kindness for them. Be gentle, be sympathetic, show mercy to others so they may become kind.

> Proverbs 14:31 says, *"He who oppresses the poor shows contempt for their Maker; but whoever is kind to the needy honors God."*

> Ephesians 4:32 says, *"Be kind and compassionate to one another, forgiving each other, just as in Christ God forgave you."*

> 2 Corinthians 6:3 says, *"We put no stumbling block in anyone's path, so that our ministry will not be discredited."*

> 2 Peter 1:5, *"For this very reason, make every effort to add to your faith goodness; and to goodness, knowledge; and to knowledge, self-control; and to self control, perseverance; and to perseverance, godliness; and to godliness, brotherly kindness; and to brotherly kindness, love."*

Again, God, through His grace, gave you His offer of salvation if you will, by faith, believe in Him. If your faith is genuine, you have received the Holy Spirit, and as He works in you, kindness becomes a virtue. Do what is right when you make a decision. Read and do His word. Resist the devil and he will flee from you. Pray and wait on the Lord. Receive directions from Him and follow exactly. Then your kindness will be seen, appreciated, and uplifting to others, and in the end, bring glory to God which is our purpose in life.

GOODNESS

Good is being kind to someone, profitable to someone, morally right, and appropriate for the occasion. To the non-believer, being good usually is to self. And if they are kind, they are kind first to themselves, then partners of many kinds, then family and friends. What they believe is a good profit is for themselves. Morally right decisions are optional if they don't break the law or if they don't get caught. Because of the sin nature they were born with, they can ignore sinful behavior or justify their behavior based on how good they are compared to their neighbor. Everyone in the world knows someone worse than themselves. Good people, I mean really good people, like moms and dads and grandparents who are kind and understanding and supportive and live by the golden rule; these people, unless they receive the Holy Spirit, will spend eternity in hell. So being good is nice, but spending eternity in heaven is much nicer!

So that describes good in the world; now let's talk about good in Christ. Good is being kind to everyone, not just those you choose. Good is profitable to God, and He will then reward you. You are slave to righteousness, so you always do what is morally right. If you fail, you quickly confess your sin, ask for forgiveness, repent, and restore your love relationship with God. You know that only God is good, and only by grace have you been saved, as you put your faith in Him. Believe in Him, not yourself. So the quality of doing good depends on the Holy Spirit in you, working to produce goodness. Good fruit that will last and be seen by others as a testimony of God's goodness. The warning: don't misrepresent Him!

Now we can look at some verses, and you can discern how much goodness you provide to the world on His behalf.

> 1 Corinthians 10:31-33 says, *"So whether you eat or drink or whatever you do, do it all for the glory of God. Do not cause anyone to stumble, whether Jews, Greeks, or the church of God, even as I try to please everybody in every way. For I am not seeking my own good but the good of many, so that they may be saved. Follow my example, as I follow the example of Christ."*

1 Corinthians 15:33-34 says, *"Do not be misled; 'Bad company corrupts good character'. Come back to your senses as you ought, and stop sinning; for there are some who are ignorant of God: I say this to your shame."*

Romans 12:9 says, *"Love must be sincere. Hate what is evil; cling to what is good."*

1 Peter 2:12 says, *"Live such good lives among the pagans that, thought they accuse you of doing wrong, they may see your good deeds and glorify God on the day He visits us."*

Titus 1:15-16 says, *"To the pure, all things are pure, but to those who are corrupted and do not believe, nothing is pure. In fact, both their minds and consciences are corrupted. They claim to know God, but by their actions they deny Him. They are detestable, disobedient and unfit for doing anything good."*

In Matthew 7:21, Jesus says *"Not everyone who says to Me 'Lord, Lord,' will enter the kingdom of heaven, but only he who does the will of My Father who is in heaven."*

That's enough verses to explain what God expects His followers to live like. The question, then, is how good are you doing, and how much goodness is in your heart? If you think you are a Christian but your actions suggest you have lied to yourself, make peace with God today! These following verses speak about how we are made alive in Christ.

Ephesians 2:1-10 says to new believers, *"As for you, you were dead in your transgressions and sins, in which you used to live when you followed the ways of this world and of Satan, the ruler of the kingdom of the air, the spirit who is now at work in those who are disobedient. All of us also lived among them at one time, gratifying the cravings of our sinful nature and following its desires and thoughts. Like the rest, we were by nature objects of wrath. But because of His great love for us, God, who is rich in mercy, made us alive with Christ even when we were dead in transgressions; it is by grace you have been saved. And God raised up with Christ and seated us with Him in the heavenly realms in Christ Jesus, in order that in the coming ages He might show the incomparable riches of His grace, expressed in His kindness to us in Christ Jesus. For it is by grace you have been saved, through faith, and this not from yourselves, it is the gift of God; not by works, so that no one can boast. For we are God's workmanship, created in Christ Jesus to do good works, which God prepared in advance for us to do."*

FAITHFULNESS

We all know faithful people; people we trust, people who are loyal friends, people who are devoted to their spouse and children and organizations. But when we talk about the fruit of faithfulness, we are talking about being faithful to God, and His plans and purposes. He is the object of our worship and praise, and it is Him in us that is at work in us to actually do His will. Don't be deceived by people who seem successful and happy and doing well, when in fact they may be spiritually dead, and what you see in their lives is a result of their efforts, and not God's. Our thoughts should be not me, but Christ in me, drawing each of us closer to Him, for His recognition and glory.

Before we can be faithful to God, we must belong to Him and obey Him, which expresses our love to Him and others. Being faithful doesn't mean you will be happy all the time. We as believers experience difficulties, trials, persecutions and even tests from God to prove or strengthen our faith, which pleases God. That is why faithful believers strive to be humble, so that our pride won't lead us to think we are better than we truly are. Faithful believers attend church fellowship, they give tithes, gifts and offerings joyfully. Faithful believers are honest, resulting in moral and spiritual integrity. We don't own stuff; we receive stuff from God and do our best to be good stewards of all He has entrusted to us. Faithful believers have a strong commitment to prayer.

> *Romans 12:12 says, "Be joyful in hope, patient in affliction, faithful in prayer."*

When God says "be", it's a command!
> Proverbs 28:20 says, *"A faithful man will be richly blessed, but one eager to get rich will not go unpunished."*

GENTLENESS

To be gentle, we are humble, soft spoken, kind, not angry, not violent, not argumentative, respectful, and loving. We can be these things on a good day or a good moment, but to actually do these things all the time we must rely on God. Thus, as His Spirit works in us, gentleness comes out of us.

> Proverbs 15:1 says, *"A gentle answer turns away wrath, but a harsh word stirs up anger."*

Therefore, be a peace maker, not an agitator!

> Philippians 4:5 says, *"Let your gentleness be evident to all. The Lord is near."*

And may I add He is watching!

> Colossians 3:12 says, *"Therefore, as God's chosen people, holy and dearly loved, clothe yourselves with compassion, kindness, humility, gentleness, and patience."*

> Ephesians 4:2 says, *"Be completely humble and gentle; be patient, bearing with one another in love."*

In 1 Timothy 6:10-12, Paul is speaking, giving Timothy, a young believer and follower of Christ, this warning: *"For the love of money is a root of all kinds of evil. Some people, eager for money, have wandered from the faith and pierced themselves with many griefs. But you, man of God, flee from all this, and pursue righteousness, godliness, faith, love, endurance and gentleness. Fight the good fight of the faith. Take hold of the eternal life to which you were called when you made your good confession in the presence of many witnesses."*

> Matthew 11:28-29 says, *"Come to me, all you who are weary and burdened, and I will give you rest. Take My yoke upon you and learn from Me, for I am gentle and humble in heart, and you will find rest for your souls."*

SELF CONTROL

Of the 9 fruits of God's Spirit, self control is the last on the list. God, knowing our weaknesses, knew that self control would come last. To unbelievers, it never comes. With His Spirit at work in our hearts, we have hope. Change can be a miracle and happen instantly, but for most, change comes slowly, even when we commit to the task. There is no greater honor known to man than to be chosen by God to represent Him in a fallen world. We are not Him, but He shows Himself to us through Jesus, who is our perfect example. As we follow Him and learn from Him, we become more like Him. His Spirit in us moves us towards self control. As you follow, you also move further away from sin and its temptations. Self control gives way to God's control, which the Bible calls being "slave to righteousness." If love has its way, you will be under control, and under His protection. And this began by God's grace, as you put your faith fully in Him, and began to obey His word. In this, God is pleased, and our lives bring glory to Him.

Proverbs 13:3 says, *"He who guards his lips guards his life, but he who speaks rashly will come to ruin."*

Proverbs 25:28 says, *"Like a city whose walls are broken down is a man who lacks self control."*

Here's another command, 2 Peter 1:6 saying, *"Make every effort to add to your faith goodness; and to goodness, knowledge; and to knowledge, self-control; and to self-control, perseverance; and to perseverance, godliness."*

All these fruits come from one Spirit, as He works in you, to equip you to do the works He has prepared for you. He plants His seed; He nourishes the seed; He continues to grow the seed; and He harvests the seed. His plan, for His purposes, in His timing, in His way, for His glory! He only asks you, or should I say, commands you to bear His fruit. He asks everyone, but most choose to say no.

If, after reading this chapter, you feel convicted that you haven't been producing good fruit, talk to God now, this very moment. Make peace with Him. He is God, and you are not. He is sinless, and you are not. He sent Jesus to die on the cross to pay the penalty for your sins, and Jesus did. Give your sins to Jesus and receive His righteousness in exchange. Believe in the fullness of God, and receive His Spirit. Then repent of your old sin nature and love your new creation in Christ, for the old is truly gone and you are now born again, you have His Spirit in you, and you now belong to Him. Seek out fellowship, seek a mentor and be discipled, ask to be baptized in the name of the Father, Son, and Holy Spirit. You've received the promise of eternal life, now start living physically and spiritually in a way that pleases Him. Death is over: life has just begun!

THE SPIRIT STORY
A Short Story

Today I'm going to tell you a story about a man who was forty years old when he became a born again believer. All you need to know about his first forty years is that he led a common life. You know that story: he was spiritually dead, slave to sin, separated from God because of his sins, prideful, boastful; darkness filled his heart, soul, mind, and his strength was physical only.

When he realized his true condition in this world, he cried out to God; made peace with God; accepted His terms of reconciliation; agreed to repent of his sinful ways; received forgiveness; and God forgave him and sealed him unto redemption. This man got saved; got born again; settled his position in Christ and became a new creation.

In simpler terms, he became slave to righteousness; he surrendered his life to Jesus; he started to follow Jesus; he started to pray in Jesus' name; and he began his life of obedience, committed to love, prayer, and reading the Bible so he could become more like Jesus.

That all took place on day one of his personal love relationship with God. On day two this story begins, as this man discovers the reality that the person now in him, the Holy Spirit, has changed everything that the man had once known. You see, the man had worldly knowledge, but no spiritual truths. He had worldly wisdom, but no spiritual wisdom. Now that true life has entered his heart, he realizes what spiritual darkness was in his life. He realized how his body now belongs to God, and that God calls his body a temple of the Lord. This man feels the change within him, and also realized adjustments need to be made so people around him will know and see and understand what has happened on his inside. So the man gets baptized, as an outward expression of an inward change. People can't see his heart, but they can see his flesh; his body. And they will now watch him closely to see if he really believes in God or not.

To describe this changed person, I want you to picture in your mind this man's body. No details other than head, arms, hands, legs, belly, and feet. In the center of this image picture his heart. Now add a light to his heart, and we'll call this light the Holy Spirit. The light is visible in your mind now, but the rest of the body is black. On the outside, this person looks the same.

Now picture in your mind the Spirit beginning to work in this person's heart. And the result of this work we call fruit, and therefore, fruit of the Spirit. Now picture this light moving to this person's head. The head now lights up, and the head's light can be seen by others. You know the look: love, joy, peace and more. So the heart is glad, but cannot be seen by others, but others see the head. The eyes bring tears of joy and thankfulness, the ears hear a new message, the eyes see hope, the nose smells something good is happening to him, and the mouth begins to praise God for what He has done. The tongue starts humbling itself and sings for joy. And the rest of the body is still dark inside, but also still looks the same outside.

So, add to this picture God at work inside the body, cleaning up the rest of the dark areas. The Spirit is always working; the head starts to communicate with the rest of the body. God calls the feet and they obey His commands. The feet start going with Jesus; to church, to Bible studies, to volunteer places of need, to mission trip places; a place called obedience. Now picture the feet in the light, because God is working there and He wants others to see where they are going.

Then the Spirit moves to the hands. The body starts doing what is right. The hands build good bridges instead of the old self that burned bridges. The hands pick up the

Bible and shows it to the head, and the head relays the word to the heart. The hands build friendships and they work hard to please his Lord and Savior. In the inside, the hands have become righteous, so they have light. In this story, picture in your mind the hands now white. Outside, people see the good works of the hands, and realize the body is changing. Realizing this, he tells them "not me, but Christ in me" has done this. Then he praises God for what He has done, so others will be drawn to His light.

In the same way, picture the legs becoming strong, so he can stand firm in his newfound faith. Grace is there. Faith allows him to move forward, even into the darkness of the world and its temptations and sinful behaviors. Again, picture his inner legs being white. Outside, people don't know how strong, but they see the newfound endurance. They first saw his love, joy, and peace, but now they also see his patience, kindness, goodness, faithfulness, gentleness, and most of all, the self-control, which they knew he never had!

So inwardly, in your picture, he is mostly white now, the heart, head, feet, hands, legs, and his arms are better. His belly will follow, and soon his inward righteousness is white. So white, he disappears! So is the story over? Hardly; it's just begun! You don't have to imagine the inward person anymore, he belongs to Christ and He will keep the inward lights shining. He is the Head. He is in the heart. He will tell his feet where to go. He will tell the hands what to do. He will equip him for ministry, and then show him where to minister. He just says "yes Lord" and do what He says. Slave? Yes, but one happy camper! And he realizes his inside is the same as the outside, and realizes how good God really is. And he worships Him. And he praises Him. And he asks that He continue to work in him for His glory, and He does!

Now is this story over? Not yet, because he still has questions, and wants answers. He begins by asking reasonable questions, and expects truthful answers, and then responds to the truth. Someone is always responsible for their choices. First, Satan is responsible for sin, lies, and spiritual darkness, for he had no truth in him. Secondly, Adam and Eve listened to Satan and chose to disobey God, so they are responsible for passing their sin nature onto all generations. Thirdly, I am responsible to choose my master. Do I want to obey Satan and his sin nature or Jesus, who offers a righteous nature? Either comes with a cost; slave to sin or slave to righteousness? You choose.

God is responsible for everything else! He is our Creator; our Judge; our Righteousness; our Hope; our Redeemer; our Everything! He will be perfectly just according to His perfect nature. He knows all things and can answer all the questions perfectly. To save you time, I will give you the answer to all questions: Jesus. The more you ask, the more you will realize this to be true!

So this story is over. Was this story about you?

FRUIT OF THE SPIRIT

Love is patient, love is kind,
Love is in your heart and on your mind.
Love does not boast; it never is proud,
Love is God, therefore, will always be allowed.
Love always trusts; always hopes; always giving.
Love is the reason you are living.

Joy is an emotion that comes from the heart,
Joy set before you can cause you to start.
Joy is a blessing that brings you delight,
Joy is a product of those living right.
Joy sometimes seems far away; then shout for it.
Joy can be complete; so don't ignore it.

Peace in the world is so hard to find.
Peace in the Spirit is hard to decline.
Peace like a river that flows late at night.
Peace that brings you pleasure inside when you are right.
Peace that can calm you, like a baby at rest.
Peace comes much quicker when sins are confessed.

Patience comes to you as you wait on the Lord,
Patience is not going too fast, yet often leaves you bored.
Patience puts love to the test; just as love gives; patience takes.
Patience takes time; time runs out; yet both correct mistakes.
Patience is a gift, spiritually speaking, that troubles might test,
Patience will give you endurance, if you wait for God's best.

Kindness has sympathy for others when they are hurting,
Kindness shows a caring heart when others are deserting.
Kindness puts a smile on a once unhappy face,
Kindness leads to kindness if you honor it with grace.
Kindness brings peace with it, as it travels down His path,
Kindness calms the angry and puts guilt upon their wrath.

Goodness alone will not save you; but a good choice will.
Goodness shows His Spirit; if you let Him, He will fill.
Goodness is an attitude, as it looks for good in others,
Goodness is a quality you find in Christian brothers.
Goodness shows mercy and kindness; not expecting gratitude.
Goodness looks for something positive, even in a bad attitude.

Faithfulness comes to us, as we keep in step with Spirit,
Faithfulness brings us closer to God as we read and do and hear it.
Faithfulness endures, even when the times get rough,
Faithfulness keeps giving, even when your days are tough.
Faithfulness is shining on a dark and cloudy day,
Faithfulness will get you through, when others pass away.

Gentleness is loving when you discipline with care,
Gentleness is bringing hope to others in despair.
Gentleness is a strength to those who are humble,
Gentleness is a good response when your world starts to crumble.
Gentleness understands when to raise its voice,
Gentleness is soft rebuke, while others make their choice.

Self control is out of control until the Spirit finds you.
Self control will hold your tongue, if tempted to be untrue.
Self control will quench your thirst; will keep your mind straight.
Self control will give you love, when all you feel is hate.
Self control takes discipline; the will to do what's right.
Self control will take some time; it doesn't happen overnight.

FRUITY OLD TREE

Jer 1:5
Now here is my story, how I came to be
I was living as soil, when God planted a seed,

Ps 149:4
My roots started growing, He gave me all that I need,
When, BOOM — I was lifted – I was born – I was free!

John 3:16
Well I broke ground and I saw the light,
I felt His Son, even though it was night,
I felt His Grace – it came pouring down
I heard Him speak without a sound.

2 Cor 5:17
My faith began, I remember the day,
There were blue skies above me – once they were gray,
Something inside me – I could feel it begin,
Guess you could say – I was born again.

Matt 5:7
Now I could see – and I could feel –
Now I could love — and I was real –
He lifted me up – and gave me a chance –
I was getting tall – even started to branch

Rom 10:15
I was still weak – though started barking about –
I kept track of my feet, but never walked them out!
I was always growing – I was never bored,
I was always giving what I couldn't afford!

Prov 16:18
But then one day – I started bearing fruit –
I was looking good — I was starting to hoot –

Rev 3:19
I guess you could say, I was feeling my pride,
When, BOOM – God was angry – and He took me aside.

John 15:5
He said – Tree, you are nothing if I leave you alone,
If it weren't for my Spirit, you'd be dry as a bone.

Ps 148:13
The fruit you've been bearin' is for others to see,
And the praise and the glory all belong to Me!

Matt 26:75	So my branches were weeping – I was feeling so sad,
	How could such good intentions end up doing so bad?
Heb 13:5	But the One who has loved me – He never would part,
Ps 23:3	I rejoiced – I repented – He restored my wooden heart.
Prov 11:30	There is life in my story, I'm now wiser indeed,
	And I share His fruit freely – there's so many to feed!
Gal 5:22	In my time – He has used me – and today life is good –
	He has stayed close beside me – like He told me He would.
Luke 14:35	That's the end of my story – well at least for today –
	I'm so glad that you listened – it just blows me away –
John 15:20	If you're bored by my message – hey – don't blame it on me!
Matt 7:17	I'm just a half-grown, wind-blown, unknown, fruity old tree!

GOD IS LOVE

Love has beginning, it never gets old,
Love has the answer, as questions unfold,
Love is our caring, down deep in our heart,
Love is forever; His truth from the start.

Love makes you happy, when you're feeling sad,
Love will protect you, from evil and bad,
Love gave us Jesus, to show us the way,
Love is His Spirit, that lights up our day.

Love is a warm tear, when we remember His story,
Love is our heartbeat, when we help bring Him glory,
Love is demanding, but well worth the bother,
Love is the warmth, when we pray to our Father.

Chapter 4
PRAYER

Prayer in the life of a born again believer is different than prayers of people who belong to the world. They who are dead spiritually have no power within them to hear and do the will of God. These worldly people are slave to sin, and their sins separate themselves from our Holy God. When this sin barrier is built, there is little hope that their prayers will be answered, unless God Himself chooses to intercede for His own plans and purposes.

My point is this, my views on prayer are given from the eyes of a born again follower of Jesus Christ. These prayers are in agreement with God's will, and the purpose is for the building up of our personal relationship with Him. So, we talk to God the Father, and we make our needs and praises known to Him, and we pray in Jesus' name because He tells us to in His word, and the Holy Spirit in us leads us, moves us, compels us, and intercedes for us when we are in need and don't know what to say.

So prayer becomes an essential part of our daily walk of faith.
    Matthew 21:22 says, *"If you believe, you will receive whatever you ask
    for in prayer."*

To the person of faith; whose love draws them close to God; whose heart's desire is to do the will of God; to that believer's prayer will come an answer, and they will know it is from Him, and they will accept the answer to be God's will for their request. Thus, knowing God and His attributes are essential in prayers which are in harmony with His nature.

We pray for things we need, not for things we want. Therefore, it is wise to begin each prayer request with the phrase "if it be Your will Lord". If our true desire is to be like Him, we should always be concerned with what God is feeling; God is doing; and God is wanting before we focus on ourselves and our wants, our circumstances, and our plans.

> In 1 John 5:13-15 God says, *"I write these things to you who believe in
> the name of the Son of God so that you may know that you have eternal
> life. This is the confidence we have in approaching God; that if we ask
> anything according to His will, He hears us. And if we know that He hears
> us; whatever we ask; we know that we have what we asked of Him."*

In John 14, verses 12-15, Jesus is speaking and says, *"I tell you the truth, anyone who has faith in Me will do what I have been doing. And I will do whatever you ask in My name, so that the Son may bring glory to the Father. You may ask Me for anything in My name, and I will do it. If you love Me, you will obey what I command. And I will ask the Father, and He will give you another Counselor to be with you forever; the Spirit of Truth."*

Then go to John 15:16-17, which says, *"You did not choose Me, but I chose you and appointed you to go and bear fruit; fruit that will last. Then the Father will give you whatever you ask in My name. This is my command: Love each other."* (Talking about other believers.)

So, to have a prayer life that is pleasing to God, we must have faith in Him; believe in who He is and what He has done and what rewards He has for those who earnestly seek Him. And to this, we are commanded to love God first and then others as ourselves, and also to bear good fruit in His name. So through our prayers, we have fellowship with God, in the name of Jesus; who is in the Father; who sent His Spirit to live in us so we might come to know His will, and do His will, in His timing, in His way, for His Glory! And in doing this, our love grows, our faith grows, our obedience increases, and our dependence on Him increases. And as a result, our confidence in Him grows, and we begin to humble ourselves before Him, and His desires become our desires, and we realize who we have become because of what He has done in us, through us, and for us, and we find ourselves worshipping Him and praising Him like never before, and He becomes our life. And at that moment, we realize we want to know Him more and more, and through prayer, we accomplish the personal love relationship that He has always wanted!

So next, let's begin with Ephesians 6:18 and see where the Spirit leads us from there. *"And pray in the Spirit on all occasions with all kinds of prayers and requests. With this in mind, be alert and always keep on praying for all the saints."*

WHAT ARE "ALL KINDS OF PRAYERS"?

1 Thessalonians 5:17 says, *"Pray continually"*

Colossians 4:2 says, *"Devote yourselves to prayer, being watchful and thankful."*

Jude 1:20 says, *"But you, dear friends, build yourselves up in your most holy faith and pray in the Holy Spirit."*

Romans 8:26 says, *"In the same way, the Spirit helps us in our weakness. We do not know what we are to pray for, but the Spirit Himself intercedes for us with groans that words cannot express."*

James 5:16 says, *"Therefore confess your sins to each other and pray for each other so that you may be healed. The prayer of a righteous man is powerful and effective."*

Mark 11:24 says, *"Therefore I tell you, whatever you ask for in prayer, believe you have received it, and it will be yours."*

Using these verses as a starting point, I conclude that God wants me to pray always, in faith, in His Spirit, in Jesus' name, with confidence that He will hear me, and grant the requests that are in agreement with His will, His timing, His plans, and His purposes.

So, what are some of the ways I can pray so I might be obedient to His word and grow in the knowledge of His will?

I'll make a list so we can identify the "all kinds of prayers" in Ephesians 6:18, and then we'll look into His word where we are told to do them. We are commanded to pray, and to not pray is called disobedience, and disobedience shows a lack of love, and love is His greatest command of all!

PRAYERS OF WORSHIP

Acknowledge who He is, the Creator of all things. Talk to Him about His attributes, for there is no other like our God. Get to know who He is, so you can worship Him more and more. In Chapter 1, we discussed His attributes. Memorize them; believe them; desire to know them, and worship Him because of who He is! Worship is the act of reverence towards God.

In John 4:21-24, it says, *"Jesus declared, 'Believe Me, woman, a time is coming when you will worship the Father neither on this mountain nor in Jerusalem. You Samaritans worship what you do not know; we worship what we do know, for salvation is from the Jews. Yet a time is coming, and has now come, when the true worshipers will worship the Father in spirit and in truth, for they are the kind of worshipers the Father seeks. God is Spirit, and His worshipers must worship in Spirit and in Truth.'"*

Remember, Jesus said He is the Truth, the Life, and the Way. His Spirit lives in us, and as He leads us to pray, we must believe He is real and that He loves us. He knows all things, and He knows what is best for each one of us. Trust in Him and He will use us for His glory!

PRAYERS OF PRAISE

God is worthy of our admiration and our approval. He deserves our worship and praise. To Him we give all glory! We recognize God's nature and we praise Him for who He is.

> Psalm 52:9 says, *"I will praise You forever for what You have done; in Your name I will hope, for Your name is good. I will praise You in the presence of Your saints."*

This psalm was written by David long before Jesus came to earth, yet remains true today as well. In 2015, we praise God for what He accomplished on the cross. We praise Jesus for shedding His blood for us so we might be saved. We praise the name of Jesus, the only name in which we may be saved. We praise Him for His word and for His grace; His love; His mercy! Read the book of Psalms. They are songs of praise to God, as our Creator, Sustainer, and Redeemer. Our praise recognizes, shows appreciation, and expresses God's greatness as Lord.

> Psalm 63:3-4 says, *"Because Your love is better than life, my lips will glorify You. I will praise You as long as I live, and in Your name I will lift up my hands."*
> He is above us in every way; praise Him!

PRAYERS OF THANKSGIVING

In our Christian thinking, we thank God with a deep sense of gratitude for all things, because it is God who makes all things good. The Bible says only God is good, and from Him all things were made good. It is mankind and our sin that corrupts His good gifts. Despite our corruption, He makes all things new and beautiful, in His time. We then are able to thank Him with sincere hearts for all that He does, all the time. We thank Him for His kindness; His unending grace; His great love for us; His patience; His mercy; His understanding; His faithfulness, and yes, His discipline in times of need, so we may come to know and love Him more!

> Philippians 4:6 says, *"Do not be anxious about anything, but in everything, by prayer and petition, with thanksgiving, present your request to God."*

The key words in this verse are "everything" and "with thanksgiving". Communicate with God on an ongoing basis, and do it all the time, with an attitude of love and thanksgiving in your heart. Not just in happy moments, but in sad as well.

In 1 Timothy 4:4, God says, *"For everything God created is good, and nothing is to be rejected if it is received with thanksgiving, because it is consecrated by the Scripture and prayer."*

All the gifts that God has given should be used to serve Him and honor Him. He gives us food, so thank Him for His gift before you eat it, and yet, honor Him by eating what you need, instead of abusing the gift through gluttony. Thank Him for His love; don't abuse His love by lusting for anything. Thank Him for the life He has given you; don't abuse His body by harming it with drugs, alcohol, unclean speech or immoral sexual behavior. He has given us the opportunity to decide; choose well!

PRAYERS OF WATCHING

Keep your eyes open, and watch what God is doing around you. When you see Him working, join Him there and be a part of His work. Watch your tongue, and speak to God about it! Watch how people use their spiritual gifts for good, then do what you have seen them do; for they are serving God. Watch for signs and wonders, and know God is near. Let your eyes see what is good and pleasing to God, and look away from all things that displease God.

Colossians 4:2 says, *"Devote yourselves to prayer, being watchful and thankful."*

Our persistence in prayer demonstrates our faith. Our faith tells us that God hears our prayers and answers them in His timing and in His ways.

In Luke 12:37, Jesus says, *"It will be good for those servants whose Master finds them watching when He comes. I tell you the truth, He will dress Himself to serve, will have them recline at the table, and will come and wait on them."*

Keep your eyes open! Jesus is coming soon, and He wants His body; His church; His bride; to be ready!

PRAYERS OF INTERCESSION

Most of the world lives in darkness and sin, and those who live in the light must intercede on their behalf to plead to God for His mercy for them. It is those who have been born again with the Holy Spirit that must pray for the lost. We know from reading John 15:16 that God chose us; we who believe in Him; but we don't know those who have not yet come into His kingdom, so we pray for all, and praise God each time a new believer is revealed to us.

And so it is; we not only intercede for the lost, but we lift up prayers for believers who become ill, tired, weary, tempted or searching for God's will for their life. We pray for our children and grandchildren, that they may find peace and joy in their relationship with God. We pray for our leaders, both worldly and spiritual. We pray for ourselves; our marriage partners; and our children's marriage partners years before they are revealed to us! Prayer pleases God, and everyone needs prayer!

> 1 Timothy 2:1-4 says, *"I urge then, first of all, that requests, prayers, intercession and thanksgiving be made for everyone. For kings and all those in authority, that we may live peaceful and quiet lives in all godliness and holiness. This is good, and pleases God our Savior, who wants all men to be saved and to come to a knowledge of the truth."*

God has chosen to include us in His work, and He tells us to pray for others, so praise Him and obey Him!

PRAYERS OF WAITING

When we are finished talking to the Lord during a session of prayer, we can extend the fellowship with Him by waiting for God's response. Sometimes quickly; sometimes not! In a world that is in a hurry and impatient, it is good to pray for all that God has laid on our hearts, and then wait for God to marinate our souls with the requests and the anticipated answers. Don't be afraid to pray for patience! The trials and tribulations that God will bring to you will make the wait seem short in comparison! But in the end, when patience arrives, you will see its value and be blessed!

> Psalm 46:10 says, *"Be still, and know I am God; I will be exalted among the nations, I will be exalted in the earth."*

> Zechariah 2:13 says, *"Be still before the Lord, all mankind, because He has roused Himself from His holy dwelling."*

Approach God reverently and wait silently to hear what He has to say. And when He speaks to you and you know what He is saying, then do it!

PRAYERS OF CONFESSION

When you belong to God, He seals you with the Holy Spirit. The Holy Spirit is alive; He is a person; He is Spirit with the personality of God; and He is God. When Jesus comes to reside in your heart, your body becomes a temple of the Lord. At times, we allow sin into this place we share with Him, and prayer is needed to clean it back up! And so we confess that what has happened is not pleasing to God; we ask for forgiveness; we receive His forgiveness; we repent from this sin; and we move forward restored through the process.

Ask God during your prayer time to reveal anything in His temple that displeases Him. Some sins enter His presence through the thoughts of your mind. Some through your eyes, some through your ears, and some may come because of your mouth! In any case, pray that you become aware and sensitive to these moments, and that God will give you the strength and power to avoid or resist these things. Persevere, for these attacks will come to you until Jesus comes for you!

> Psalm 139:23-24 says, *"Search me, O God, and know my heart; test me and know my anxious thoughts. See if there is any offensive way in me, and lead me in the way everlasting."*

PRAYING SCRIPTURE

Reading God's Word back to Him honors Him. Open your Bible and declare His truth by reading it aloud to yourself, to others in the room, or to God above who hears your prayers. Let God know through reading that His word is valuable to you, and that you want the whole world to hear it! Sometimes I mix Scripture prayers and prayers of confession together. I'll be reading, and His Spirit convicts me of my guilt in this passage, and I'll immediately confess my error and restore my relationship with Him, then go back to reading more.

As you pray, declare His word boldly! Speak the verses that reflect your faith in Christ. Let your heart rejoice as you talk to the Lord about His great love for you! Worship Him and praise Him for making His word alive in you!

> 1 Timothy 4:13 says, *"Until I come, devote yourself to the public reading of Scripture, to preaching and teaching."*

> Acts 17:11 says, *"Now the Bereans were of more noble character than the Thessalonians, for they received the message with great eagerness and examined the Scriptures every day to see if what Paul said was true."*

Want your character to be more noble? Pray Scripture; go to church; hear the preached word; learn from those who teach. Then, go home and read that which was preached and taught in your Bible, and reprove what you heard is true and accurate!

PRAYERS OF PETITION

These are our personal needs. God knows what our needs are, but He also tells us that we have not because we haven't asked Him. So ask, and you shall receive. Of course, pray that it be His will that you receive the answer to your request, and accept the fact that He might say "no" or make you wait until He's ready to answer.

> Matthew 7:7-8 says *"Ask and it will be given to you; seek and you will find; knock and the door will be opened to you. For everyone who asks receives; he who seeks finds; and to him who knocks, the door will be opened."*

The Bible was written to believers, and though non-believers who have not received the Holy Spirit cannot discern what it is saying, some Scriptures can be understood and applied by whosoever chooses to read it. This verse is one of those. To a lost, spiritually dead person, they can ask for God's forgiveness and receive it. They can seek truth and find Jesus and the story of the cross. And the door, Jesus, will offer the free gift of eternal life, and if they receive Him, they are sealed with the Holy Spirit until the day of redemption.

For true believers, ask and receive forgiveness, blessings, ministry opportunities, more grace, more love, more spiritual gifts, healings, protections, and exceedingly more!

PRAYERS OF SINGING

Praise and worship God through moments of singing. At church, in the shower, while you work, while you drive down the road!

> Psalm 100:2 says, *"Worship the Lord with gladness; come before Him with joyful songs."*

> Psalm 101:1 says, *"I will sing of Your love and justice; to You, oh Lord, I will sing praise."*

> Ephesians 5:19 says, *"Speak to one another with psalms, hymns, and spiritual songs. Sing and make music in your heart to the Lord."*

> James 5:13 says, *"Is any one of you in trouble? He should pray. Is anyone happy? Let him sing songs of praise."*

You can't sing what you don't know! If your radio station doesn't play praise and worship songs; change the channel! If the book you are reading isn't worth singing about; sell it and buy a hymnal! If your heart is not joyful, fill it with the Holy Spirit, and the Spirit will produce in you love, joy, peace, patience, kindness, goodness, faithfulness, gentleness, and self control!

PRAYER TIME OF LISTENING

God gave us ears so we could hear Him. We can also listen to our heart. We can listen to or ignore what our senses tell us. We can smell trouble, and we can listen for advice on how to avoid it. Our reflexes can cause us to react to something harmful, but we should learn to listen to what they are saying before they grow weary or go away. Listening to God is like hearing these examples.

We should listen to what the Spirit is saying to us. We should hear and obey what God says to us. We should listen to our pastor, our elders, our teachers, and other believers. Why? Because God speaks to us through His word, His Spirit, and His people. He is in control, and He places people in our path to minister to us.

> In John 10:27, Jesus says, *"My sheep listen to My voice; I know them, and they follow Me."*
>
> In Luke 10:16, Jesus says, *"He who listens to you listens to Me; he who rejects you rejects Me; but he who rejects Me rejects God the Father who sent Me."*
>
> James 1:22 says, *"Do not merely listen to the word, and so deceive yourselves. Do what it says."*
>
> James 1:19-20 says, *"My dear brothers, take note of this: everyone should be quick to listen, slow to speak, and slow to become angry, for man's anger does not bring about the righteous life that God desires."*
>
> Proverbs 18:13 says, *"He who answers before listening; that is his folly and shame."*
>
> Proverbs 12:15 says, *"The way of a fool seems right to him, but a wise man listens to advice."*

When we listen during our prayer moments, we should not be surprised when God speaks to us or when our prayers are answered. Not because we deserve, but because He loves us beyond our understanding, and despite ourselves, He wants us to receive blessings in abundance!

Meditate on what is good and pray you can become like that. Ponder, think, listen and believe the things of God. You will be amazed how much closer you will be drawn to Him, and in the process, become more like Him!

So, you see now how important prayer is, and how you can actually spend a lot of time there daily. Prayer is a command from God. When we choose to spend more time in fellowship and prayer with Him, we are showing our love to Him.

> James 3:17 says, *"The wisdom that comes from heaven is first of all pure; then peace loving; considerate, submissive, full of mercy and good fruit, impartial and sincere."*

To pray is a wise thing, and how you pray will reflect the true condition of your heart. Are your prayers about your will or God's will?

> James 5:16 says, *"The prayer of a righteous man is powerful and effective."*
> What makes us righteous? JESUS.

THE POWERS OF PRAYER

Pray, and all good will survive, He will make you alive;
You will know life is good.
Pray, and your heart will be blessed, all His words you'll digest;
You will be understood.
Pray, and His light will shine true, He will surely enlighten you;
You will see as you should.
Pray, and He will hear your heart, you will know where to start;
As He promised He would.
Pray, and His truth is at hand, you will know where you stand;
You will know He is good.
Pray, and His will shall be done, He will help everyone;
His inspiration is beyond good!
Pray, and His peace will be found, it will be all around;
And you will feel good.
Pray, and each day brings delight, there is peace in the night;
You will live as you should.

PRAY FOR MISSIONARIES

It's mission time, around the world; prepare to meet your Lord!
Are you prepared, to do your part? How great is your reward!
The call is out; the time is now, it's time to make your plans,
You've known before, but put it off; our spirit now demands!

Everybody knows the need; I've seen it on your faces,
How hard it is, to find the time, that time alone erases,
If we miss, this chance to serve, we may not have another,
Use us Lord, and lead the way, so we may reach our brother.

Equip us with, the tools we need, then send us on our way,
Prepare a team, give each a part; some lead; some follow; some pray.
We want to serve; we want you back; we want to do it now!
Please bless us Lord, and give us strength; we know You'll show us how.

I feel Your love, as it flows through my heart,
And I understand Your affection,
Our passion for missionaries, has only begun,
Prepare us, and give us direction.

Chapter 5
THIS THING CALLED REPENTANCE

I think that everyone who knows the English language has an understanding of what repentance is. The word itself implies that there is a feeling of regret for one's behavior, whether it be something you have done or not done. This regret causes sorrow, and brings with it a desire to turn away from this thing and move away from it.

As a believer in Jesus, the importance of repentance is much greater. It is more than a feeling of regret or sorrow; it is a command of Christ! It requires action, which requires a proper choice. It becomes a matter of obedience to God's Word, which challenges the heart on the issue of love.

In Luke 13:3, Jesus says, *"But unless you repent, you too will all perish."* Without repentance, there is no forgiveness of sins."

In John 14:15, Jesus says, *"If you love Me, you will obey what I command."*

In Matthew 22:37, Jesus says, *"Love the Lord your God with all your heart and with all your soul and with all your mind."*

Again, this is not a good suggestion but a direct command! Therefore, repentance becomes an act of love, revealing the true condition of our heart.

So, whether you are a believer in Christ or not, we can agree on some truths. The word repentance does exist; it has meaning; it can be understood; and it requires action if we choose to apply it to our lives. Here lies the challenge which we must understand.

Because we enter the world alive in the flesh but spiritually dead, we are not only slave to sin, but the Bible teaches that we must be "born again" to receive the Spirit of the Lord, thus receiving the power to overcome the sins that cause us to be in need of repentance.

So, let's address the persons who have not yet come to repentance. We, as believers, refer to those persons as non-believers; not believing in Jesus as their Lord and Savior. Believers in Christ are those who, though still sinners, are forgiven by grace, as we place our faith in what Jesus accomplished on the cross. So non-believers are referred to as those who are lost in the world, still needing a savior. In a place of darkness; a place filled with sin; hopelessly destined for the place called Hell.

So, to approach the issue of repentance, we must first come to a place in time when we realize that we are sinners, in need of a Savior. Then, we must seek information that convinces us who that Savior is. Once God reveals these truths to us, we can then make a wise decision to accept this Savior, Jesus, into our hearts and begin our personal love relationship with Him that will change our lives forever.

So, to the non-believer, you must be willing to repent. Because of your sin nature, you are slave to sin. You may have a desire to be a better person, but you lack the power to conquer the behavior you display, which causes you grief, sorrow, or sadness. If you have reached this point in your life, when you realize you can't succeed on your own efforts, there is good news. Start by reading Romans, Chapters 5 and 6. Once you confess your sins; ask for forgiveness; receive His forgiveness and receive the Holy Spirit, you now have the power to overcome the world!

> In 2 Corinthians 5:17, *"Therefore, if anyone is in Christ, he is a new creation; the old has gone, the new has come!"*

We are no longer slave to sin! We now have power over sin, and also, the power to repent! Sinless? No, but forgiven! Therefore, no person will go to everlasting hell because of sin, for Jesus died once for all sin. The blood of Christ, shed to cover the penalty of sin, which was death, is for all people. Even so, He gives us a choice to receive Him or reject Him! If you search your heart and realize your life is not pleasing to God, take the time right now to make peace with Him! By faith, you can enter into His kingdom, and when you do, He will do in your heart what no other person or thing can do!

> To the non-believer, the Bible says in 1 Corinthians 2:14 that, *"the man without the Spirit does not accept the things that come from the Spirit of God, for they are foolishness to them, and he cannot understand them, because they are spiritually separated from truth."*

If you can believe, do so! Allow God to transform your mind! Allow Him to make all things new! You will be eternally blessed!

THIS THING CALLED REPENTANCE

This thing called repentance, implying regret,
A heart filled with sorrow for sin you have met.
A turning from evil that place you enchanted,
A drawing from Jesus, that Jesus implanted.

Decision, decision, a choice must be made,
Your sin for His righteousness is offered in trade.
Though willing and ready, your nature enslave,
The Spirit from Jesus is needed to save.

Decision completed; forgiveness achieved,
The Spirit with power has now been received.
In Christ, new creation, the old nature gone,
Position established; relations now on!

Learn and choose obedience, and learn to pray,
Not just in the morning but throughout your day.
Be reading the Bible, be patient and kind,
Be thoughtful in Spirit, as He transforms your mind.

Be righteous and humble, be fruitful and love,
Acknowledge your blessings from God up above.

This thing called repentance will visit again,
Sin will still find us; we still live as men.
Press forward, be tested, be tempted, be true,
Be faithful to Jesus, who once died for you.

One nice thing about being the author of a poem is that I can communicate to others exactly what I meant or what I want the reader to understand about what my poem is saying.

In verse one, I define repentance from a Christian point of view. The acknowledgement of sin, the heartfelt emotion of sorrow and regret, and the understanding that to please God, one must turn away from sin and move towards Jesus and His righteousness knowing also, since the Bible teaches that no one seeks after God, it is God who draws us to Himself.

In verse two, you have a choice to make. Choose light or darkness. The Bible says they have nothing in common. Jesus says, *"choose life, so that you may live."* Since you must be born again with His Spirit, you must be dead in your sins spiritually, lacking the power to overcome the sins of the world. Do you choose to be slave to sin or slave to Christ and His righteousness?

In verse 3, you made the right decision and chose life. Jesus is now Lord over your life. You belong to Him; you trust Him; you love Him; you have His peace; you now have hope; eternally! You have a heavenly Father; you live in Christ and He lives in you; His Spirit has become your Counselor, your Comforter, your Mentor. You have now been sealed unto redemption, as mentioned in Ephesians 4:30 and Ephesians 1:13-14.

Having now the power to repent, continue to do so! I say continue because the process started when God drew you to Himself and caused you to turn from sin long enough to make a good decision. Now, through obedience and faith and God's grace, you are ready for a personal love relationship with God. To repent was a huge move in the right direction. Now, go, and identify yourself through baptism, and learn obedience as you follow Christ.

Wow! Look what happened in verse 4! Because you were willing to repent, God opened your eyes to truth, and showed you the way back to Himself. Now that you are able to do what is right, do it! Show your love for God by learning and obeying His commands. Prayer is essential as you develop your relationship with God. Pray in Jesus' name and believe what you pray for is God's will, and you will receive it. Allow the Holy Spirit in you to do His work, and bear good fruit for His glory!

We, the body of Christ, have a perfect example to follow in Jesus, the Christ. He is perfect; we are forgiven, but still fall short and sin. When sin finds us, don't ignore it or try to hide it. Confess it, receive His forgiveness and move on, once again doing this thing called repentance.

> And as the Bible clearly teaches in 1 John 1:9, *"If we confess our sins, He is faithful and just and will forgive us our sins and purify us from all unrighteousness."*

> So I ended this poem thinking about 1 John 2:6. *"This is how we know we are in Him: whoever claims to live in Him must walk as Jesus did."*

THE MAN WHO NEVER REPENTED
A Short Story

This is a story about a nice guy that I met in high school, and after graduation, we fell out of touch for forty years. But as fate would have it, we ran into each other at an all school reunion a few years ago and have since renewed our friendship. I find him to be even nicer today than he was in our youth, and remember, he was nice then. Well, at least compared to me!

Rather than recall the high school days in detail, I think I'll share the most recent conversations we have had during a week we spent in Hawaii with our wives. We have a habit of reliving our special moments of our youth over and over, and over again until we convince ourselves it must have been fun! Our stories are that way, and though our recollections may be blurry, the events did happen; clouded sometimes by things beyond our control, like alcohol, drugs and people who we can't remember if they were there or not, but it's the story that matters, not necessarily the details of the story.

Our first evening in Hawaii was really fun. After a day of sunshine, and drinks, we went to a nice dinner club where we had steak and lobster and more drinks. And so the evening went, great weather, good food, good company, and plenty to drink! Between the laughter of one story of our younger days came the laughter of another story, and you can imagine our wives' joy of hearing these funny stories of behavior which we forgot to share with them in the past. We recalled our first dates, our first keg parties, and the usual stuff like car accidents we survived, and a few stories about those who didn't. Yep, we covered a lot of ground that first day, and it was good.

On day two, we woke up late with hangovers, but nothing a couple of aspirin and a Bloody Mary couldn't fix. Being on vacation, we ate a brunch; laid in the sun; went out to supper; and partied the same as the night before. Oh yeah; same drinks; same stories; but this time our wives pointed out the discrepancies, and yet, they were just as funny!

So day three comes; hangovers; three pills; took two Bloody Marys just to get to lunch; we missed our brunch. Laid in the sun; slept in the sun; got sun burnt; went to supper; and partied just like before. Only this time, when we laughed over our same stories, we argued with our wives when they corrected our stories, and they got mad and went to the rooms. We stayed and shared some new stories we didn't want our wives to hear. At some point, our waitress woke us up and told us it was time to go home. We did!

So day four comes; wives go to breakfast and wake us up when they get back from the beach. We get up, take our pills, drink our two Bloody Marys, and asked our wives to go shopping while we catch up on our rest. They did, and we got up in time for supper. We're on vacation; we decide to drink something local. Coconut this, pineapple that, tropical this, paradise that; and we were laughing and having fun again. Our wives got silly, and started telling their untold stories. We got mad and had a few choice words to share, then left them sitting there. When the bars closed, we all ended up back at our rooms. We each slept in our own bed and nothing was said.

Day five comes. Around noon, we quietly shower and have a cup of coffee, looking out the window at the ocean. Sure was peaceful. The ladies decided to spend the day at the beach, and they left. We decided to spend the day golfing, and we left a note so they would know where we were. After golf, we had supper at the clubhouse, had a few drinks, and spent the evening complaining about our wives. Our wives decided to take an evening dinner cruise, and spent their evening complaining about us. When the bars closed, we all arrived at our rooms, argued about how much money we all spent, and went to our beds.

Day six comes. We wake up and discover we've all spent our cash, and our credit cards were close to being maxed out. We decide to spend the day at the beach. We got sun burnt again, this time worse where we peeled from the first time. We grabbed a hamburger at the snack bar and went to our rooms. We did watch TV for a while, then went to our beds to sleep.

Day seven. Checked out of our rooms; took a taxi to the airport; waited two hours to board our plane; we can't afford souvenirs; it took about eight hours flight to land near home; said our goodbyes for a great trip; drove another hour to get home. Unloaded the car; set the alarm to get ready for work the next day.

Well, like I said, that trip was a few years ago and we still recall each day as it happened, and we still laugh when we relive that once in a lifetime vacation. We call each other on our birthdays, talk about the good old days, and say we'll do it again someday.

Well, my friend died last week, and I went to his funeral. The church was packed; he was a well liked guy, and a nice guy too! And as the stories were shared about his life, we laughed a little, and realized we will miss him. Then the preacher starts in, and the place gets quiet. The preacher said God loves us, but sin separated us from Him. He said the wages of sin is death, and that we all have sinned and fall short of His glory, which I figured out was heaven. Yet Jesus was born to die on the cross to pay the price of sin for whosoever believes in His name.

The preacher didn't know my friend, but he said my friend's wife told him that he was not a believer. My friend thought he was doing fine, and that he figured he hadn't done enough bad things in his life to deserve hell. After all, God is love, and love wouldn't punish a nice guy!

I was in agreement with my friend, right up to the funeral. But then, the preacher explained the attribute of God known as justice. Equal to God's love; it is God's responsibility to judge all people fairly and justly. Those who never made peace with God would be judged guilty. Those who never accepted Jesus as Lord would be judged guilty. Those who never received the Holy Spirit of God would be judged guilty. And Jesus knows those who didn't choose Him!

It was a sad crowd leaving that church, for we all knew our friend well, and we knew he had never changed his ways or his thinking, and why should he? He was a nice guy! For me, I believe the preacher knew what he was preaching about. On my way home, I stopped and bought a Bible. I started reading the New Testament, which someone said was the new covenant of grace.

It took me 15 hours to read from Matthew to Revelation. Then I went online and read the questions and answers of other believers and seekers. Last night, I realized the Bible was accurate and true, I confessed my sins and asked for forgiveness, and asked Jesus to give me eternal life. I received love and peace the moment I believed and obeyed His word for the first time. Tomorrow, I'm going to church to thank God for what He has done.

My wife thinks I'm crazy, but seeing the sincerity on my face, she said she will go to church with me tomorrow. Pray for both of us as we begin our new life in Christ.

ONE VOICE

If you were a teacher, what would you want most?
To be a good mother, or be a good host?
If students dislike you, would you still set them straight?
Could you live with the burden, if you tell them too late?

Mistakes made sincerely, are still judged as wrong,
If we don't sing the same notes, do we sing the same song?
If sins are committed, the truth must be taught,
The battles of life, can't be won until fought!

The tongue can confuse us, so let our hearts seek,
What good are our answers, if the truth we don't speak!
As parents, we're equal; our answers must jive,
We share what we're given, to keep love alive.

So look to the future, and not at the past,
Our children are growing, and much, much too fast!
A family is watching; let's help them to see,
Our song is worth singing, in sweet harmony.

FINDING PEACE

Somewhere, in the darkness, a lonely man cried,
Some tears on his face, and some hidden inside.
He has no tomorrow, this man of the night,
Just sorrow and heartbreak, with no help in sight.

Nobody could reach him, he lived all alone,
His family deserted; his address unknown.
He drank dirty water, he slept on the street,
No friends to protect him; a sad man to meet.

So there, in the gutter, this worthless man lay,
He cried out in anger, with no choice, but to stay.
Then up walked a stranger, so meek and polite,
Who said "If you're willing, I'll show you the light!"

I wasn't the stranger, but I'm glad he arrived,
Without love and caring, no one would survive,
A born again Christian, who lives without fear,
God is pleased someone told him, now his future is clear.

REPENT AND BE SAVED

For hundreds of years now, the Bible we've known,
It offers salvation, though not on its own.
We must come to know God, and believe in His Son.
A marriage in heaven, will make all three one.

A pretty nice offer, but hard to believe,
Has something been hidden, up somebody's sleeve?
We've heard other stories, and few turned out true,
This could be a gimmick, from out of the blue!

Forget all those critics! Stand up to their lies!
A choice is in order, be it foolish or wise!
Put faith in His story, His grace is His gift,
Be part of His glory; your spirit He will lift!

My heart heard His offer, I accepted His grace,
My soul is now heading, for a much better place!
I wanted salvation; He saved me, it's true,
Now I'm one of His children, feeling gracious and new.

Chapter 6
COMMITMENT

Commitment carries the same meaning in the Christian life as it means in the world. You make a decision to do something, then you follow through with that pledge or thing. If you say you will, you are committed. You volunteered or pledged your support, and when you actually do this thing, you fulfill your commitment.

From the Christian point of view, your commitment to follow Christ is a life changing decision, and it is a decision that you commit to from that moment on. So, once you become a Christian; born again; you have committed an act of surrender, which binds you through faith to God. God's grace saved you; faith in Jesus set you free from the bondage of sin; and the Holy Spirit sealed you and enables you to overcome the world.

> 2 Corinthians 5:17 says, *"Therefore, if anyone is in Christ, he is a new creation, the old has gone, the new has come! All this is from God, who reconciled us to Himself through Christ, and gave us the ministry of reconciliation."*

You committed your life to Him; you pledged your life to Him; and He accepted your offer, and in return, He sealed you with His Holy Spirit; and you now are committed for life. The Spiritual death you once were slave to has been defeated, and spiritual life has begun. Now you are committed to live like and become like Jesus.

> 1 John 3:9 says, *"No one who is born of God will continue to sin, because God's seed remains in him; he cannot go on sinning, because he has been born of God."*

Believers are not perfect. They will choose to sin from time to time, but this verse says we who have been born again will not choose sin over righteousness. And if we do, we restore our relationship quickly by confessing our sins, and through repentance from these sins, we move forward in grace.

We are born of God when the Holy Spirit lives in us and His Spirit gives us new life in Jesus. This new life changes our hearts and transforms our minds to make us more like Christ.

So how much commitment does God expect from us? We are for Him or against Him. We are sealed or not. He wants us hot or cold; for lukewarm is gross and soon spit out. He wants all! Heart; soul; mind; and strength imply the whole body. He bought us with a price and He expects us to produce fruit that lasts.

So here's the answer you need to understand; but with God all things are possible. Don't give up! Don't lose hope! Don't lose faith! Don't stop loving and caring! Persevere, and let grace go with you down your path that Jesus made and you are following!

You've made the right choice to receive Jesus as Lord, now make daily choices that please God, like committing to pray, committing to fellowship, committing to reading the Bible, committing to becoming like Christ!

Put aside self-centered ideas and desires and seek out God's plan for your life. If you truly have His Spirit, you have all you need to live a righteous life, for greater is He who is in me than he who is in the world. He in me is God, and he who is in the world is Satan, demons, and non-believers. You have spiritual power, so use it! Believe it to please God. Use it for God's glory! Share it to testify to the world about God's great love; that they too may come to know eternal life and escape the second death! Believers are more than conquerors, they are ambassadors for Christ!

> Ephesians 6:10-18 says, *"Be strong in the Lord and in His mighty power. Put on the full armor of God so that you can take your stand against the devil's schemes. For our struggle is not against flesh and blood, but against the rulers, against the authorities, against the powers of this dark world and against the spiritual forces of evil in the heavenly realms. Therefore, put on the full armor of God, so that when the day of evil comes, you may be able to stand your ground, and after you have done everything, to stand. Stand firm then, with the belt of truth buckled around your waist, with the breastplate of righteousness in place, and with your feet fitted with the readiness that comes from the gospel of peace. In addition to all this, take up the shield of faith, with which you can extinguish all the flaming arrows of the evil one. Take the helmet of salvation and the sword of the Spirit, which is the Scripture. And pray in the Spirit on all occasions with all kinds of prayers and requests. With this in mind, be alert and always keep on praying for all the saints."*

WOW! There's your commitment to Christ. Once you became a "born again believer in Christ", this commitment became a command! Don't take it lightly or think it is just good advice. DO IT!

THE BEAUTITUDES

Position, money and authority on earth are not qualifiers to serve Christ in His kingdom. What He wants is heartfelt, faithful obedience towards Jesus and the examples He showed us while on earth. Pride, religious activities and disobedience will not be tolerated. We, as followers of Jesus Christ, are not to expect fame or fortune, but we are warned that we will face mourning, trials, tribulation and persecution as we follow Him and His ways. Jesus asks us to lay down our lives for the good of others.

Our goal in following Jesus is to obtain hope and joy that only those who know Jesus in a personal way can experience. Not because of our circumstances but because of Him, what He has done in the past; what He is doing for us today; and what He has waiting for us in the future.

> Matthew 5:3 Jesus says, *"Blessed are the poor in Spirit, for theirs is the kingdom of heaven."*

This verse speaks about the humble, which speaks against the prideful, and the desire to be independent. To become humble, we must submit ourselves to God. We resist temptation and overcome evil. Jesus is our hope and joy in times of sorrow or mourning.

> Matthew 5:4 Jesus says, *"Blessed are those who mourn, for they will be comforted."*

While the world seeks after happiness and personal successes, Jesus asks His disciples to share in other people's grief and mourning, and He will bring us peace, comfort and joy when we need it.

> Matthew 5:5 Jesus says, *"Blessed are the meek, for they will inherit the earth."*

As the world seeks after money, power and prestige, Jesus tells His followers to be satisfied with what He gives us. He's all we need, and He rewards those who earnestly seek Him.

> Matthew 5:6 Jesus says, *"Blessed are those who hunger and thirst for righteousness, for they will be filled."*

As the world seeks after personal wants and desires for their own pleasure, Jesus says to be satisfied with Him. He becomes our righteousness, and we are to become like Him. Go beyond satisfied and desire total victory over sin.

> Matthew 5:7 Jesus says, *"Blessed are the merciful, for they will be shown mercy."*

While the worldly want to appear strong and powerful at all cost, Jesus is saying we should have compassion on those who are weak or less fortunate than ourselves. So believers in Christ show love to all, and trust that God's strength and power and grace is all we need.

> Matthew 5:8 Jesus says, *"Blessed are the pure in heart, for they will see God."*

Those who have deceitful and evil hearts will manipulate, lie or deceive to obtain the desires of their hearts. Their wants are greater than the needs of others. They think they deserve all they can get, and usually work hard to get their way. Jesus teaches to do what is right at all cost, and do it because it pleases Him, not for personal gain or recognition. The pure heart has Jesus there, and will have eternal life in heaven.

> Matthew 5:9 Jesus says, *"Blessed are the peacemakers, for they will be called sons of God."*

The world is always at war against itself, and worldly people jockey for power and control over everything. The world wants to lead. The world wants to win, and will do whatever it takes to achieve their goals. Worldly peace is about self; my comfort; my joy; my toys; my position; my attitude; my well being. Jesus says, "Obey Me and I will give you peace." So Christians strive to reconcile their differences and avoid conflict, even if their rights are taken or given away for Christ's sake. And their reward is the kingdom of heaven.

> Matthew 5:10 Jesus says, *"Blessed are those who are persecuted because of righteousness, for theirs is the kingdom of heaven."*

Many will say they are Christians, yet when trials and tribulations come, their commitments to Christ vanish. They are weak minded and only hope to gain something from God at NO COST. True believers persevere through their sufferings and become stronger in their faith because of them. These believers are already experiencing God and His love and His provisions for eternal life.

> Matthew 5:11-12 Jesus says, *"Blessed are you when people insult you, persecute you, and falsely say all kinds of evil against you because of Me. Rejoice and be glad, because great is your reward in heaven."*

Your reward: Jesus; eternal life; heaven; glorified bodies; never ending peace and joy!

COMMITTED TO DARKNESS
A Short Story

I've always like committed people. When I was young, I played a lot of baseball with my friends and we played all summer, meeting at 10:00 every day at the park. Then we'd pick teams and play until we ran out of energy. I can still remember how I hated the wimps who overslept, or were just plain lazy. And some would decide to swim instead of playing ball; I called them liars. Yesterday, they said they'd be there but today they didn't show up! Then there were the hypocrites, who said they liked playing ball, but liked just about everything else better, so were no shows most of the time. Then there were the cry babies, the ones who showed up most of the time, but cried when they fell down, or their team was losing, or their pants got grass stained; well, you know the ones. And then came the "fair weather" kids. If it starts to rain, they quit. If the wind blows, they quit. The sun's too hot; I'm thirsty; I'm whatever! Bottom line, out of the 14 kids who committed to be there to play, we usually had 6 we could depend on.

My friend, who was always there, is the friend this story is about. Because he always practiced, he became the best player in our neighborhood. He seemed to be good at everything, but he liked baseball the best. As he grew older, he was the best pitcher in Little League, then the best in High School, then the best at College, then finally got drafted by the Minnesota Twins organization and signed a contract for 30 million dollars for 5 years. He was committed.

He spent 5 years in the majors and had a great record. In the off season, he liked to party. He owned a nice 10 million dollar home, a million dollar yacht, and a small plane with his own landing strip. He traveled a lot when he could, and had a different woman with him on each trip, which he found exciting. That was the good news.

Then came spring training, and time to sign a new contract. He was caught speeding in his fancy sports car and was arrested for going 120 mph in a 70 mph zone. They found cocaine in the back seat and was charged with possession. During further investigation, the authorities discovered his yacht was being used to run drugs from Cuba to Miami, and his boat was confiscated. While waiting trial, his attorney bailed him out of jail, but things just got worse. Before he could go to trial, he got into an argument, someone pulled a gun and two people were shot to death. He was arrested again; the Twins organization released him, and while in jail, his home was sold at auction to settle all his other debt. He went to trial, was found guilty, and was committed.

He served his five years in prison, and when he got out, he had nothing left but his sad story. He was so committed, and yet, he chose to commit his life to a life of sin and darkness. He tried to change his ways, but he never recovered from his mistakes. Depression took over, and he turned to drinking to ease the pain. He met a woman at a party one night and they drove to Vegas and got married. He committed his life to her, and after about a year, she drove him crazy, so he was committed to a mental institute. While there, he committed adultery with another patient. Shortly after his divorce, he committed suicide.

I was there at his funeral, and when I was asked to say a few words, I did. I simply said this, "He was a fun guy and the most committed man I've ever known." In all our years of friendship, we never once thought about spiritual things, until that moment when I realized he was committed to death.

Not a happy ending, but not so uncommon these days. As for me, I still like committed people, and I've committed my life to finding out the truth about spiritual things I've never known. I bought a Bible the other day, and someday I'm going to read it. I don't want to end up like my friend.

THE NEW BELIEVER

Welcome to my heart; let Your Spirit in,
Forgive me for my past; repent me from my sin.
I have seen Your light; I've been born again,
I am here to serve; show me where and when.

When the evening comes; teach me what to say,
Guide me in my thoughts; guide me as I pray.
With You, I am strong; without You, I am nil,
You are my cup in life; it's up to You to fill.

Treat me as Your child; feed me what is right,
Do with me at will; keep me close in sight.
Lead me to Your door; answer when I pray,
Call me, I will hear; teach me, I will stay.

A POEM OF COMMITMENT

Do I have anything, that you still desire?
Can I do anything, that still lights your fire?
If I go anywhere, without your embrace,
I will have nothing left, but tears on my face.

Is there a spark of life, left in your heart?
Is there a memory of, "till death do we part"?
We've let this bitterness, get in our way,
Let's search for happiness, and let's start today.

If Jesus is Lord of us; it's time to obey,
Not just in all we do, but in all that we say,
Let anger dissolve in us; replace it with love,
We've struggled with everything; now heal from above.

The Spirit is here in us, but we can't let Him grieve,
Forgiveness is offered us, but we must receive,
Repentance is clear enough, yet something we choose,
If we hold on to sin, in the long run we lose.

So if there is hope for us; if broken can mend,
Give grace as You heal us; speak to us as Friend,
Whatever it takes, is how we will pray,
For You are the Potter and we are Your clay.

Chapter 7
THE BODY OF CHRIST

The Bible makes it clear that there is, and always will be, only one true body of believers, and the Head of this body is Jesus, who gives life and discipline to each part. Jesus is the one who is in control, and He is the One who has a master plan for His Creation, and He chose and built His church to accomplish His purposes and plans as He wills it. And when the work is finished, there will be rest for all who followed Him and overcame the sinful life of the world. Heavenly days ahead!

In these end times in which we live, people don't want to hear that JESUS is the only way. They want to believe in themselves, or some other way that makes sense to them, but the Bible declares they will forever be separated from the one true God. Therefore, it is essential that you come to know the right God; the Triune God we have already discovered in chapter one of this book and in all of the collected books known as the Bible. Knowing the one and only God, we can confidently place our faith in Him. Some will say they believe, but only to find out later they believed a lie! Don't be deceived and don't deceive yourself! Truth is revealed to those who ask; so ask the right person! Jesus.

There is a saying I like, and it goes like this: A person talks about what they know in their head, but they live their life by what they believe in their heart. Is Jesus in your heart or just in your head? So let's look at a few Scriptures that will give you a clear picture of "The body of Christ"; "His church"; "His bride"; and "our hope".

> 1 Corinthians 12:12 says, *"The body is a unit, though it is made up of many parts, and though all its parts are many, they form one body; whether Jews or Greeks, slave or free; and we were all given the one Spirit to drink."*

> 1 Corinthians 12:24-26 says, *"God combined the members of the body and has given greater honor to the parts that lacked it, so that there should be no division in the body, but that its parts should have equal concern for each other if one part suffers, every part suffers with it; if one part is honored, every part rejoices with it."*

> 1 Corinthians 12:27-28 says, *"Now you are the body of Christ, and each one of you is a part of it. And in the church, God has appointed first of all apostles, second prophets, third teachers, then workers of miracles, also those having gifts of healing, those able to help others, those with gifts of administration, and those speaking in different kinds of tongues."*

When a person enters into a personal love relationship with God, He sends you His Holy Spirit as a gift and seal of His ownership. With His gift comes at least one, often more, special gifts to enable you to do the ministry or ministries He has or will call you to. We call them spiritual gifts. It is essential that all believers identify their personal gift, and they pray for opportunities to use them. Otherwise, you are not doing your part as a function of His body. If God says look, He is talking to the eyes. If you are the feet; wait for further instructions!

If you are a believer but never have known your spiritual gift, there are many books and tests you can find to help you in your discovery. Internet has much on the topic. I'll simply list a few so you are aware of the many available. Leadership, preaching, teaching, administration, wisdom, faith, service, mercy, giving, hospitality, knowledge and evangelist to name some. The important thing is to work with your gift, doing God's plans, in God's timing, in God's way, so He will receive all the glory for what He has accomplished through you and the rest of His body.

> Ephesians 4:1-5 says, *"As a prisoner for the Lord, then, I urge you to live a life worthy of the calling you have received. Be completely humble and gentle; be patient, bearing with one another in love. Make every effort to keep the unity of the Spirit through the bond of peace. There is one body and one Spirit, just as you were called to one hope when you were called. One Lord, one faith, one baptism, one God and Father of all, who is over all and through all and in all."*

> Ephesians 5:29-30 says, *"After all, no one ever hated his own body, but he feeds and cares for it, just as Christ does the church, for we are members of His body."*

> Colossians 1:15-20 says this about Jesus, *"He is the image of the invisible God, the firstborn over all creation. For by Him all things were created; things in heaven and on earth, visible and invisible, whether thrones or powers or rulers or authorities, all things were created by Him and for Him. He is before all things, and in Him all things hold together. And He is the Head of the body, the church; He is the beginning and the firstborn from among the dead, so that in everything, He might have the supremacy. For God was pleased to have all His fullness dwell in Him, and through Him to reconcile to Himself all things, whether things on earth or things in heaven, by making peace through His blood, shed on the cross."*

To the non-believer, this verse is saying you need Jesus in your life because He is your only hope to escape hell.

To the believer in Christ, these verses say it all! God the Father is awesome, powerful, perfect in every way, holy, loving, faithful, just, and exceedingly more! And yet, all the fullness of God is "in Jesus"! WOW! Even God the Father put all of Himself into His Son, so that through His Son, Jesus, all glory and praise could return to Himself!

> James 2:26 says, *"As the body without the Spirit is dead, so faith without deeds is dead."*

We have talked already about how all people are born into this world spiritually dead, and therefore, must be born again to receive life through His Spirit. And faith in anyone or anything other than in Jesus will produce nothing but dead works. Remember how God compares our most righteous works of the flesh to dirty rags. Our bad works, then, aren't much worse! The works that God accomplishes in us or through us, because of Him, these are the works that please God. Our faith is in Christ, and our works are not our own, but His.

> Romans 12:4-5 says, *"Just as each of us has one body with many members, and these members do not all have the same functions, so in Christ, we who are many form one body, and each member belongs to all the others."*

Just as all church attendees are not born again followers of Jesus Christ, keep in mind that the body of Christ in your town does not all attend the same fellowship building. We who are members of the true body are told to have a special love for other believers in His body. So, for the sake of unity within the body, we pray for each other; we love each other; and we encourage one another.

Satan and his followers will be around to cause divisions in your fellowship and in the body of Christ. There are plenty of issues that divide our fellowships into fifteen locations instead of one, and this will continue to the end of time. That being said; we can love one another just as Christ does. Jesus also said that those who are not against Him are for Him. Therefore, we move forward; focusing on Jesus; following Jesus; obeying Him and trusting Him to work out all things to those who love Him.

All persons who have put their faith and trust in Jesus have another thing in common: His Holy Spirit. We who are in Christ and Him in us are new creations. Knowing and believing this causes us to live lives worthy of His calling for us. Our goal as Christians is to become more and more like Jesus until He calls us home. Until that moment, we need each other to be effective in ministry to the lost. Let's pray that Jesus will call our feet together so the whole body can see what God sees, and hear what we've all been saying since our new nature took over, and together be one.

Ephesians 4:14-16 says, *"Then we will no longer be infants, tossed back and forth by the waves, and blown here and there by every wind of teaching and by the cunning and craftiness of men in their deceitful scheming. Instead, speaking the truth in love, we will in all things grow up into Him who is the Head, that is, Christ. From Him the whole body, joined and held together by every supporting ligament, grows and builds itself up in love, as each part does its work."*

In John 17:11, Jesus says, *"I will remain in the world no longer, but they are still in the world, and I am coming to You. Holy Father, protect them by the power of Your name, the name you gave Me, so that they may be one as We are one."*

Luke 14:33 says, *"In the same way, any of you who does not give up everything he has cannot be My disciple.*

John 14:15-24 says, "If you love Me, you will obey what I command. He who does not love ME will not obey My teaching. These words you hear are not My own; they belong to the Father who sent Me."

When we talk about the body of Christ in reference to the church, we are talking about the spiritual body, made up of all believers, in which Jesus is the Head. Now Jesus could also be considered the heart of the body as well, but Scripture focuses on leadership and God's will, and Jesus is clearly the brains of the body He built. It is His Spirit that brings life to believers.

We have already read the verses which describe His body, and we looked at verses describing who will not be in heaven representing His body. We have also looked at verses encouraging us to work together in unity, as we are not all feet, or hands, or arms, or legs, etc. And we also looked at spiritual gifts that make ministry possible.

Given this much information, why will most people not want to surrender their lives to Christ, or if they say they want to, why can't most do it? It's a matter of faith. We find it hard to believe in what we cannot see. Yet, that is not the only answer. People who saw Jesus perform many miracles still lost interest in Him and returned to the comforts of home. Then there is a thing called instincts, then intuition, then reflexes, then circumstances, then IQ, then wisdom or foolishness, then knowledge of good and evil, then to those, add man's will that resists commands, and temptations that interest our curiosity, and above all those things, the real battle: the spiritual realms which rage all around us and have power to take our souls to places we can't even comprehend. Then other factors like liars, deceivers, and believers of lies who convince us they know what we don't know. And then, since we are born into darkness with our sin nature, we are slaves to sin, which means spiritually dead. To all of these, add the fact that most of those in darkness don't even realize it!

So here is the only answer to all our problems: "But with God, all things are possible." Only God is perfect and worthy of heaven. Only God is sinless and could die as the perfect Lamb on God, which covers sin. Only God could send His Holy Spirit to declare us righteous, and only God could come up with a perfect plan to save mankind from death. And this one God did all these things! Do you believe in this God who revealed Himself as a Triune God so we might see how His plan might be possible? Only one way; His way! Only Jesus saves, and you must believe that He is God, and that He rewards those who earnestly seek Him.

So why did it take me 46 years living in darkness before I could even consider Jesus as Lord? No excuses, but grace covered my life until my eyes were opened! And this miracle I can only praise God for! My faith? He gave me that too! My choice? He chose me. My love for Him? He first loved me. Turning back? Never. Slave to righteousness? Yes. Am I grateful? Yes, eternally!

THE BODY OF CHRIST – THEN AND NOW

First His spirit was; then creation was spoken through Him.
Then by Spirit; to the virgin, who then knew Him.
Then by flesh; as His chosen mother bore Him.
Then the cross; where death was waiting for Him.
Then the grave; where the cost of sin laid on Him.
Then new life; as He conquered death upon Him.
Then ascension; as He showed direction to Him.
Then His spirit; sent to save and seal through Him.
Then the church; who by grace and faith believed Him.

Now the spiritual body; all who trust and have received Him.
Now the new creation in Christ; eternal life; which is more Him.
Now His fruit; which by the way is good; and it's for Him.
Now the cost; as we lay our lives down to serve Him.
Now the life; show His grace; we didn't deserve Him.
Now the hope; just as He left, He's coming back; glorify Him;
Now the millennium; a thousand years where many will try Him.
Now the end judgment; when you wish you didn't neglect Him.
Now to the lake of fire; the many who chose to reject Him.

Then and now; it was always about Him.
Then and now; you are with or without Him.

Chapter 8
LIVING FOR GOD – THE LIFE OF OBEDIENCE

As you can tell from the title of the chapter, I believe the two headings are linked closely together. We cannot live for God without obeying His word, nor can our obedience to Him be without love and joy. We don't obey because we have to, but because we want to. Choices must be made every day, and we make them based on what we believe to be pleasing to God. This is true if you are a born again follower of Jesus Christ. If you haven't made the decision to accept Jesus as Lord, your daily choices are made to benefit yourself, or your family, or your plans, or your desires. Based on your sinful nature, these choices are normal, acceptable to the world, truthful to the best of your understanding, and yet, have nothing to do about pleasing God.

So as I share a few verses with you, what you hear and see in these verses will help you discover your true nature. If you are living in sin and are okay with your choices, your sin nature separates you from God. You are still slave to sin and are spiritually dead. If you hear God's Word and find yourself obeying His teachings and commands, you have become a new creation in Christ and, though a slave to righteousness, you are living for God and are waiting to go home to be with Him. Then come those who have deceived themselves. They say one thing and do another. They choose church, but avoid ministry commitments. They own Bibles but seldom read them, and when they realize sin is close to home, they hide it instead of confessing it and repenting of it. They have many things in life, but seldom ask God what He wants them to do with them. They travel, but seldom to serve God by sharing the good news. They have reasons why they made their choices, but have no excuses when their choices were bad. They are the religious, but do their will daily instead of God's will for their life. These people think they are ok with God, but their choices reveal a hard heart, and living for God and obedience to God's Word are options, not commands! This gray, lukewarm place is not where you want to be! Jesus may say He never knew you!

> Ephesians 2:4-5 says, "But because of His great love for us, God, who is rich in mercy, made us alive with Christ even when we were dead in transgressions – it is by grace you have been saved."

> 2 Corinthians 5:17-18 says, "Therefore, if anyone is in Christ, he is a new creation, the old has gone, the new has come! All this is from God, who reconciled us to Himself through Christ, and gave us the ministry of reconciliation."

John 14:15-17 says, *"If you love Me, you will obey what I command. And I will ask the Father, and He will give you another Councilor to be with you forever; the Holy Spirit."*

1 John 5-3 says, *"This is love for God; to obey His command. And His commands are not burdensome."*

John 14:23-24 says, *"If anyone loves Me, he will obey My teaching. My Father will love him and make our home with him. He who does not love Me will not obey My teaching. These words you hear are not My own; they belong to the Father who sent Me."*

Mark 12:30 Jesus says, *"Love the Lord your God with all your heart and with all your soul and with all your mind and with all your strength. The second is this: 'Love your neighbor as yourself.' There is no commandment greater than these."*

In Matthew 22:37-38 Jesus says the same, *"Love the Lord your God with all your heart and with all your soul and with all your mind. This is the first and greatest commandment."*

In Luke 10:27, Jesus says the same, *"Love the Lord your God with all your heart and with all your soul and with all your strength and with all your mind, and, love your neighbor as yourself."*

Romans 6:16-18 says, *"Don't you know that when you offer yourselves to someone to obey him as slaves, you are slaves to the one you obey; whether you are slaves to sin, which leads to death, or to obedience, which leads to righteousness? But thanks be to God that, though you used to be slaves to sin, you wholeheartedly obeyed the form of teaching to which you were entrusted. You have been set free from sin and have become slaves to righteousness."*

Romans 6:19-23 says, *"I put this in human terms because you are weak in your natural selves. Just as you used to offer the parts of your body in slavery to impurity and to ever-increasing wickedness, so now offer them in slavery to righteousness leading to holiness. When you were slaves to sin, you were free from the control of righteousness. What benefit did you reap at that time from the things you are now ashamed of? Those things result in death! But now that you have been set free from sin and have become slaves to God, the benefit you reap leads to holiness, and the result is eternal life. For the wages of sin is death, but the gift of God is eternal life in Christ Jesus our Lord."*

Matthew 12-30, Jesus says, *"He who is not with Me is against Me, and he who does not gather with Me scatters."*

It is impossible to be neutral about Christ! Anyone who is not actively following Jesus and His ways has chosen to reject Him. To refuse to follow Christ is to choose to follow Satan, his demons and his deceived.

James 5:12 says, *"Above all, my brothers, do not swear; not by heaven or by earth or by anything else. Let your "yes" be yes, and your "no" be no, or you will be condemned."*

Satan is the father of all lies. Non-believers are slaves to sin and lie to themselves and others all the time. Religious people have the appearance of righteousness, but lack the power to overcome lies, half-truths and stories with no truth in them. True believers who have come to know and love God have received the Holy Spirit and now have the power to choose what is right and then do it.

So, where are you at in these Scriptures? Slave to sin with no righteousness in you? Slave to righteousness and living the life God has planned for you? Or somewhere in a place you call the middle? Maybe the gray? Maybe deceived and haven't seen the truth yet? Maybe just a disobedient Christian? A free spirit believer? Let's pray together right now and ask God "Am I for you or against you"? We'll close this chapter with these verses.

Matthew 25:31-33, Jesus said, *"When the Son of Man comes in His glory, and all the angels with Him, He will sit on His thrown in heavenly glory. All the nations will be gathered before Him, and He will separate the people from one another as a shepherd separates the sheep from the goats. He will put the sheep on His right and the goats on His left.*

Matthew 25:41-46, Jesus continues, *"Then He will say to those on His left, 'Depart from Me, you who are cursed, into the eternal fire prepared for the devil and his angels. For I was hungry and you gave Me nothing to eat, I was thirsty and you gave Me nothing to drink. I was a stranger and you did not invite Me in, I needed clothes and you did not clothe Me, I was sick and in prison and you did not look after Me.' "They will answer, 'Lord, when did we see You hungry or thirsty or a stranger or needing clothes or sick or in prison, and did not help You?' "He will reply, 'I tell you the truth, whatever you did not do for one of the least of these, you did not do for Me.' "Then they will go away to eternal punishment, but the righteous to eternal life."*

The sheep – God's chosen; followers of Jesus; believers in Jesus; true Christians; the body of Christ; the church; the saved; the born again.

The goats – Those who follow Satan; the deceived; the evil; those living in darkness; those who rejected the Holy Spirit; the lost.

THE OBEDIENT FAMILY
A Short Story

Once upon a time, we believed there were families out there in the world that were great examples in which we, the normal people, could model our lives after. You know the ones; the Waltons; the Ingalls; the Crosbys; and the Cleavers. Situations, challenges, problems, issues, all believable, yet all overcame because they were good people and that's what happens to good people and good families; things work out for the good in the end. All is well. Lesson learned and victory was always the end result.

Then we realize we were fed a cleverly written story of make-believe characters in a make-believe world. To help sell the story, they hire real live actors, who help deceive us into believing these stories are possible, and maybe true. We enjoy the story so much we actually love the characters; we even give awards to the actors who gave the story life. Almost idols or heroes!

Then comes the truth. Our favorite actors and actresses get off the stage and begin to spend their money. They have affairs and it makes headlines around the world. When they divorce, we hear about it. When they kill we are shocked. When they rape or molest, we can't believe it! When they commit suicide, we feel sorry for them and wonder why they did it? They acted as if life was the "American Dream", but in the end; for the actors; life was truly a nightmare! Their true value to humanity and God was nothing! They made their millions lying and deceiving, and acted as if they deserved something in return!

That being said, my story has nothing to do with the actors, storytellers, or the perfect family. This story is about the average family who loved God so much that they obeyed what the Bible said to do. And despite their trials, temptations, circumstances and relationships, they remained true to their Lord and Savior, Jesus Christ. This is a good, truly good, story.

This was not my family from birth, though I have come to know them well as part of my family when I became a born again follower of Jesus Christ. Because of our relationship and fellowship over the years, I can share this about them.

Pa was born in the late 40's and grew up on a farm in Iowa. His parents survived the great depression, and though they lived a modest life, there were many good memories. Pa worked hard at farming until his parents died, then sold the farm and started a small appliance repair shop. While attending a church potluck in 1975, Pa met Ma, and a year later they got married.

Ma grew up in the same town, but was raised in a wealthy home. She was attractive, talented, homecoming queen, party girl; if you can imagine; and was given a new car for graduation. Despite these advantages at youth, and despite a scholarship offer, she chose to remain at home to help serve in the Red Cross organization. She was an attendee of her local church, but never really got involved in the choir, missions, teaching, or that kind of stuff.

But in 1976 when she got married, things changed a bit. Pa encouraged her to join the choir because of her lovely voice, so she did. Pa had become a Sunday school teacher and asked Ma if she would help him, so she agreed, and enjoyed teaching.

In 1980, Jim, their first child was born. In 1982, they gave birth to Sue, their first daughter. In 1984, while pregnant with their third child, Ma was involved in a car accident and the child was lost. Ma spent the rest of her years in a wheelchair, but never lost her faith in God, or her family. She lived to see both Jim and Sue graduate, then died in 2001 from a blood clot and other complications.

Pa lived another 14 years, dying in January of 2015. He never got to retire, but he never talked about that day anyway. He was content in his position in life, and felt blessed to be part of Ma's life and time spent with his son and daughter.

Neither Jim nor Sue ever got married, but are both serving as missionaries in Africa. I keep in touch, and consider myself "uncle", though only through friendship. I worked for Pa for 30 years, then bought the appliance business when he died. I'm close to retirement myself, but will stick around a little longer if it be God's will. I could have shared more about this family, but it would take a book to share their story of grace, but one page is enough to reflect their love for God and the life they led for Him.

You see, life isn't about how much I can get from the world, but instead, it's about how much God can bring to the world through us. It is not me, but Christ in me that touches the world in a lasting way.

This family gives us hope as an example of what God can do with an obedient attitude of gratitude. The Bible says "This is love to God, that you obey My commands." Real families have struggles in this fallen world, but true believers overcome the world and desire to please God, even to the point of dying to self, for the good of the gospel of Jesus and the cross, for God's glory!

OBEDIENCE

Trust and obey, every day, in every way; then stay.
Love to obey, in every way, every day; then remain that way.
Hear His command, understand, do what is right; rejoice.
Speak what is good, be understood, make things right; your choice.

See the right path, walk the path you see; see the light.
Do the right thing, be right when you do; do only right.
Trust in His name; then do the same; Trust Him only.
Believe what He says, then do what He says; Follow Him only.

Confess when you're wrong; return to the right; repent; He restores you.
Faithful is He; the right you will see; His Father adores you.
The way He makes clear, He draws you near; He knows you.
The truth is He'll care, your sins He will bare; He chose you.

Holy is He, who now reigns in me; I follow Him gladly.
Not all will proclaim, in His holy name; death will come sadly.
But you need not fear, His love is still here; believe Him today.
Time will soon end, you can still be His friend; or be sent away.

HELP ME OBEY

Don't let the sin in my life define me.
Don't let the love of my life decline me.
Touch me, lead me, and draw me back when I roam.
Jesus, I'm trusting you all the way home.

Don't let the thoughts in my mind deceive me.
Don't cause the things in my heart to grieve me.
Hold me, scold me, and teach me the way I should be.
Jesus, it's You I want others to see.

You are the truth, You are the way.
You are the reason I'm living today.
You are Creator of all that we see.
You are the Spirit in me.

Don't let the darkness around me defeat me.
Don't give the devil the time to deplete me.
Know me, show me, and be there wherever I go.
Jesus, You're all a person should know.

Don't let the times of my life confuse me.
Don't let the moments in life abuse me.
Love me, feed me, each moment of every day.
Lord Jesus; change me and keep me that way!

"IT" IS LOVE

Consider the journey, then live it; today.
Follow your heart, then give it; away.
Reach out to others, then pass it; through.
Cast off your burdens, then class it; true.
Seek what is truth; then believe it; enjoy.
Find all life's answers; then receive it; employ.
Ask for your future; then share it; free.
Hold open your eyes; then bare it; see.
If thinking is challenged; then launder it; then.
Consider commitments; then ponder it; again.
Know where you're going; then move it; there.
Declare what you have; then prove it; share.

A SHORT LOVE THOUGHT

God placed this thought in my heart.
He gave the words to reveal it.
He chose this moment, before it would start.
He waited, until I could feel it.
Love is the message, He wants you to hear.
Doing His will, when you hear it.
Knowing; believing; and perfectly clear.
Following closely His Spirit.

Chapter 9
THIS PLACE CALLED HELL

If hell exists, we should be able to find it in the dictionary. So I looked, and here is what I found. There are three descriptions offered in Webster's Encyclopedia of Dictionaries. First, it describes hell as the residence or dwelling place of the damned. Secondly; the everlasting place of punishment of the cursed. And thirdly; a place of misery or torture. So, from the world's point of view; hell exists, it is everlasting, and it is home for those who are damned.

From God's perspective, if hell exists, He would speak the truth about it in His word: the Bible. So I looked in the Bible, and found the word hell used in 54 verses. So, according to God's Word; God created a place and called it hell. There is a purpose for this place, and God will judge who gets to spend eternity there. The good news for all mankind is this, you didn't get to choose your sin nature; Adam chose to sin and passed that on to everyone else through his blood; but you can choose to break away from your sin nature if you choose Jesus as your Lord and Savior. And He will save you from hell, which is where eternal death will exist.

The Bible also refers to hell as a pit, a common grave, a world of the dead, Hades, outer darkness, eternal fire and lake of fire, eternal judgment and eternal damnation. I found 23 of these verses, but I'm sure there are more. I'm not making an exhaustive list of all verses about hell, but simply stressing a point. Hell exists. God will judge your heart and send you there if you haven't been born again in Christ. Do not be deceived!

So let's look at a few of the verses that apply to hell and see who will be there. As you read with me, consider if you might be in danger of being sent there. Keep in mind that you were born spiritually dead and inherited your sin nature. Unless you realize where you're at today, you may not see where you will be tomorrow either! Spiritual death, which is being separated from God because of sin, starts out from birth, but can be treated! The treatments are costly, but effective. In fact, those who come to believe in Jesus have a 100% chance of eternal life. Those who never come to the cross and Jesus are dead already.

> John 3:18 says, *"Whoever believes in Him is not condemned, but whoever does not believe stands condemned already because he has not believed in the name of God's one and only Son.*

> Matthew 25:41 says, *"Then Jesus will say to those on His left; depart from me, you who are cursed, into the eternal fire prepared for the devil and his angels."*

Revelation 20:10 says, *"And the devil, who deceived them was thrown into the lake of burning sulfur, where the beast and the false profit had been thrown. They will be tormented day and night forever and ever."*

So that takes care of Satan and the fallen angels who chose to follow him in hopes of becoming gods themselves. They were wrong!

In Matthew 13:40-43 Jesus says, *"As those who followed the evil one, Satan, are gathered and burned in the fire, so it will be at the end of the age. The Son of Man will send out His angels, and they will weed out of His Kingdom everything that causes sin and all who do evil. They will throw them into the fiery furnace, where there will be weeping and gnashing of teeth."*

So now Jesus adds to judgment all those who reject Jesus Christ as Lord and Savior. By not choosing Christ, you have already chosen Satan and his fate! Free will doesn't always turn out free. So now you understand why I teach about our freedom to make choices, but I don't tag on "free"! Choose freely, but consider the costs of your choice!

Back to Revelation 20:11-15 where the dead are judged. At this judgment, books are opened, and God sees the good and evil deeds of all men recorded during their lives on earth. We are not saved by works or deeds, but works can be seen as clear evidence of a person's actual relationship with God. God judges the heart, and is looking for Jesus in it. Without Jesus covering our sins, only sin will be seen, and the penalty for sin is death!

Starting at verse 11, *"Then I saw a great white throne and Him who was seated on it. Earth and sky fled from His presence, and there was no place for them. And I saw the dead, great and small, standing before the throne, and books were opened. Another book was opened, which is the book of life. The dead were judged according to what they had done as recorded in the books. The sea gave up the dead that were in it, and death and Hades gave up the dead that were in them, and each person was judged according to what he had done. Then death and Hades were thrown into the lake of fire. The lake of fire is the second death. If anyone's name was not found written in the book of life, he was thrown into the lake of fire."*

The lake of fire; hell; is the ultimate destination of everything wicked; Satan, the beast, the false profit, the demons, death, Hades and all those people who did not place their faith in Jesus the Christ.

In 2 Peter 2:4-10 it says, *"For if God did not spare angels when they sinned, but sent them to hell, putting them into gloomy dungeons to be held for judgment; if He did not spare the ancient world when He brought the flood on its ungodly people, but protected Noah, a preacher of righteousness, and seven others; if He condemned the cities of Sodom and Gomorrah by burning them to ashes, and made them an example of what is going to happen to the ungodly; if He rescued Lot, a righteous man, who was distressed by the filthy lives of lawless men who tormented Lot in his soul because of their unrighteous deeds that Lot heard and witnessed, if this is so, then the Lord knows how to rescue godly men from trials and to hold the unrighteous for the day of judgment, while continuing their punishment. This is especially true of those who follow the corrupt desire of the sinful nature and despise authority."*

God is love, but never forget that God is JUST. He rewards those who earnestly seek Him, and He also rewards those who do not! The reward for sin is death, and God's judgments are perfect and justly made! Bottom line; be on God's side!

Proverbs 11:4 says, *"Wealth is worthless in the day of wrath, but righteousness delivers from death."*

The day of wrath is judgment day, but your opportunity to receive Christ as Lord and Savior may come quickly, perhaps tomorrow, and catch you by surprise! It is the nature of sinful man to put off decisions that will cost him something dear to him. But since our days are numbered and we don't know our last day, some decisions have more urgency than others. Or should I say "should have" more urgency! I could say your decision is a matter of life or death, but I would rather you hear it from God Himself. The Bible says you have not because you haven't asked! Ask God for truth, and He will deliver. Pray for wisdom and understanding, and you will receive.

I want to share two more verses, then we'll move on. Sometimes the best way to picture in your mind a place like hell is to compare it to a picture of heaven. The Bible gives us insight on both heaven and hell, so let's learn from God's Word what we can expect to see.

First, we read 2 Corinthians 6:14-15, *"Do not be yoked together with unbelievers. For what do righteousness and wickedness have in common? Or what fellowship can light have with darkness? What harmony is there between Christ and Satan? What does a believer have in common with an unbeliever?"*

In your mind, link these together: Jesus; light; righteousness; born again believers in Jesus Christ and truth. In the same way, link these together; Satan; darkness; sin; lost; lies and unbelievers of the Truth, the Life and the Way.

> 1 Corinthians 2:9 says, *"No eye has seen, no ear has heard, no mind has conceived what God has prepared for those who love Him."*

But we can imagine, and we can ask the Holy Spirit to stretch our imagination to allow us to see a deeper faith in Christ, who will give us a deeper understanding of hope and joy that come from Him. Start with knowing that God is good. Then imagine real good. Then imagine really, really good! Now imagine indescribably good and rest there. Now you are ready to begin to know; to praise; to worship; to love; to desire Him! Now He will draw you closer; and your vision and hopes will become real; and you will be humbled by His greatness; and you will discover that heaven is near; and to know you will one day be there is enough. Then more than enough! Heaven is our home if you believe in Jesus, and when we arrive, we will know our place, and it will be perfect!

> Revelation 21:4 says, *"He will wipe every tear from their eyes. There will be no more death, or mourning or crying or pain, for the old order of things has passed away."*

This place is heaven, and God promises it to all who believe in His Son.

So now you have a clear picture of heaven, only it's infinitely better! Now you can imagine the place that has nothing in common with it...Hell.

We read a few of the 75 verses in the Bible describing this place that non-believers will call home for eternity. Now let's imagine the worst we can about this place, because if heaven is incomprehensible, so is hell.

Start with the obvious, the pain, physical pain that never goes away. No pills; no drugs. You're thirsty, but only warm, dirty water to drink that smells stagnant. Mental pain, recalling all the times when you knew you should have done what was right, but you chose wrong. You know your children watched you most of your life, and probably followed your example, but you haven't heard from them forever, and you get more depressed. Spiritual pain, realizing your unbelief in God kept you from a love relationship with Him. Now you only have yourself and others like you to follow. You realize the blind are leading the blind and no one knows where they are going, but you follow anyway, because there is nowhere else to go. And you get more depressed.

Darkness, yet some vision as a result of the fires that keep you warm, or should we imagine hot? No stars; no sun; no moon; no sky; no lakes. No mountains; you live in the valley of death; which also means no fishing; no hunting; no boating; no skiing. No snow; but there will probably be cold places that will drive you back to the hot places. Sorrow; regrets; anger; every moment of your death; forever!

God took all the good animals home, but left hell with the rest. Snakes, rats, mosquitoes; all hungry! Beasts that attack and cause fear and pain, but you have eternal bodies, so you survive; over and over again like a nightmare that keeps coming back to haunt you.

There are toilets, but no water to flush them. Probably smells. There are clocks, but they don't work, and if they did work, they wouldn't mean anything anyway. No vacations; you have no other place to go; depressing. There will be building supplies to build your own house, but the thieves steal them from you, then thieves steal from the thieves, then you become a thief to get them back, and someone else steals the supplies from you again, so your dream house never gets built!

I have a pretty good imagination, but you've heard enough to get the picture. We can't imagine only evil beings having hearts with only evil thoughts, with evil minds, with evil intensions towards everyone! On earth today, we have the Holy Spirit at work; we have church people doing churchlike stuff. We have many people trying to please God through works. We have friendly people doing friendly stuff. But in hell; God and all His church is gone! Without love, joy, peace, patience, kindness, goodness, gentleness and self-control working together, everything changes! To the extreme opposite!

Love turns cold and into bitterness and hate. Joy turns into sorrow, sadness, hopelessness and tears of regret. Peace turns into anger, rage, violence and war. Patience turns into fear; kindness melts away into rude bitterness. Gentleness turns into scars of violence. Self-control is lost and you become slaves of circumstances, which in hell is bad.

In hell; kind old ladies; moms who took good care of their families; dads who worked hard and led peaceful lives will be miserable. Rich people who had everything they desired and poor people who were satisfied with little will also be miserable. Even when most of these people arrive in hell one day, they will become like Satan and his followers and all the other evil people, because they rejected the Holy Spirit and Jesus who offered eternal life in heaven to all who would believe.

Now you know how much God hates sin, and He is justified for His anger! Remember His sovereignty; His holiness; His righteousness! And yet His love was offered to everyone, and most chose to hold onto sin! Now you know how much He loves you! Now you remember the cross, and if you can, repent if you haven't!

Remember, God's ways are not our ways! A wise person will at least learn how to please God if he decides to follow Him! But a fool will remain in his sin nature and hope God changes His mind and saves everyone! Some things never change, and God is one of those things! He is the same yesterday, today, and tomorrow, and His word is an attribute you can believe in! His plan; His way; in His timing; for His purposes, for His Glory!

JOURNEY INTO DARKNESS ... HELL
A Short Story

In the beginning of this place, Satan found himself cast into this new world of darkness. It had been Satan's lifetime dream to be god over all, and finally, the moment he had longed for was real. Many demons stood around him waiting for instructions of what to do next. And around the demons, billions of humans, all wondering what would happen next. At that very moment, Satan, the father of all lies, stepped forward and began to speak.

He knew there would be many questions asked by his followers, like what happened to the sun and stars and moon? For it was obvious to everyone they were standing in a huge cave-like place. The only light was from fires burning in holes in the rock, but no one knew what was burning. And what is that terrible smell that seemed to be everywhere? And where did all the children go? And where are we going to find food to feed so many?

So Satan went on to explain what must have happened to all of them, starting with the obvious and then continuing forward to establish a plan of action to begin this new time together. For each question raised, Satan had a good answer, and the crowd believed him.

And so it was, a new kingdom was established and Satan declared himself god of this kingdom, and called this place "Death". For death simply meant separated from, and this kingdom was now separated from the original place where life began.

That place where the self-proclaimed God of the Trinity enforced all His rules and regulations and drove most people crazy for most of their lives! Praise Satan, for he set us free from that life and we are finally free to do whatever we want, whenever we want! So Satan told them to go find food, and everyone realized they were hungry and did as they were told.

It didn't take long before people realized that there were only four sources of food in their kingdom. There were snakes, large spiders, rats and bats. Satan knew that people would quickly get tired of eating the same stuff over and over, so he told his people that he would find better food for them and that they should not worry. Upon hearing this, the people believed Satan, and began looking forward to the moment when real home cooked meals could be enjoyed.

Now Satan, knowing he had just lied to his followers, decided he had to come up with a plan of action that would satisfy his followers. So he called them together and began to explain what they had to do next. Satan knew many things from his past, and though he didn't want to anger his followers, he realized he would have to be honest to these people so they would understand their need for him. So Satan continued speaking, and the people continued to listen.

Satan spoke on, saying, "I have some good news and some bad news to tell you. The good news is that in this kingdom we will live forever! There is no more need for watches or calendars, for this day will never end! And your bodies will never die; you will live here forever and ever! Which means that I, Satan, will always be your lord and you can worship me forever and ever!" And the crowd went silent, as they realized the bad news was yet to come. So Satan, taking advantage of the silence, continued, "The bad news is that we really are trapped in this place forever and this place is called Hell."

Immediately upon hearing this, fear raged in the hearts of everyone! It was as if their first moments in this place had been some sort of dream and all of a sudden they had awakened from this dream and it was a real nightmare! Everyone was naked! They realized they were thirsty, but there was no water! They were cold, but there was no heat. There were fires burning like eternal flames, but there was not warmth! No one had a home to rest in, for they realized they had been resting on the ground. The sounds of millions of people screaming and crying sent a chill down the spines of everyone. Fighting broke out everywhere. Blood was shed, bruises formed on every body, but when the fight was over, they realized they were immortal! Pain, tears, sorrow, hopelessness, anger, rage, yet they would heal and do it again and again and again!

And the critters realized they were the only food in Hell and they become fearful and angry too! They gathered together and plotted to attack these humans before humans came after them!

So the snakes gathered together and joined forces. Every snake teamed up with others to form an army! In all, their combined mass was ten feet deep and one hundred miles long and they, too, became hungry! Some had teeth; some could swallow a man's leg in one gulp! Some had poison; some could wrap around you and crush bones! And they moved towards the place where the people were.

And the rats came together and formed another army. They too were angry and hungry and agreed not to eat each other, but only humans. So they began to move towards the humans. Like a cloud moving across the sky, they moved onward.

The spiders gathered also and there were so many it looked like a mountain sliding towards the humans. Some would bite, some would poison, and some would build cobwebs strong enough to hold ten people without breaking. Some had already learned to crawl into the ears and mouths of people and lay their eggs inside their stomachs!

And the bats were just as violent! Some had rabies, some could bite hard enough to bite off a finger, some were large enough to carry off a human to eat on later, and some could get into your hair so firmly they could not be removed unless you cut all your hair off! When they came towards the humans, it looked like a solid flock of blackbirds ready to attack!

Satan saw these four armies coming and told his followers to calm down and listen. We will fight and defend our homeland and drive these critters away! And as we drive them away, we will continue after them until we find a better place to live!

Before a battle plan could be made, the critters were upon them! Chaos broke out as billions of critters fought with billions of humans! Fear was everywhere and the battle continued for what seemed like forever! The battle ground was moving, but not dying. Blood became food. Battered critters were eaten, yet they continued to come. Critters bit and chewed on humans like locust in a corn field, but no one died!

Constant fear. Screaming and crying got louder with each passing moment, with no hope in sight. Those who were attacked by the snakes began to fear them greatly! Those who were attacked by the rats feared them greatly! Those who were attacked by the spiders began to fear them greatly, and those who were attacked by the bats grew to fear them greatly. And so fear overwhelmed them all! But Satan, being clever by nature, came up with a plan and formed four armies. He shared his plan with the people and they believed it would work, so they agreed to obey.

The people who feared the snakes wouldn't have to fight the snakes! They could fight against the bats, which seemed to them much better. The people who feared the bats then could fight against the snakes. After fighting flying critters for so long, fighting snakes seemed much better. The people who feared the spiders would be gathered to fight the rats. This too seemed better! And so it was, the people who feared the rats could fight the spiders, and all seemed better!

The new battle plan was working! When the critters realized that the humans no longer feared them, they became fearful themselves and quickly retreated! As each army continued after their enemy, stopping to eat and rest, then they pressed onward. They battled and chased the critters for what seemed like forever!

The wounded made their way back to the original place they had called Death. In that place, Satan was waiting to comfort them with his stories of past victories. Food and water in this place was no longer an issue. They learned that there was nourishment in their scabs, so they ate scabs two or three meals a day. Water wasn't fresh, but plentiful. The water was salty, but they grew to like it. People swam and made human deposits in it on a regular basis, but one good thing about an eternal body is that no matter what goes in or out, you survive!

All of a sudden, the sound of screams of rage came over the kingdom. It had seemed like forever the last time such fear and turmoil came to this place. A cloud of bats swarmed against the people. Snakes slithered over the ground and onto the people. Spiders were everywhere and webs captured many people. Rats ran quickly through the people; hungry, thirsty, fearful! The battle had returned! Each army had chased their enemy all across the kingdom until they chased them all the way back!

Once again, every person who feared the snakes has to confront them again and their fear grew so greatly, that they began to run away! When the snakes realized that the people were afraid of them again, they quit running away from the army and began to chase them again. The snakes were in control and the last time their screams could be heard, well, seems like forever!

And so it was with each army! The rats chased the people who feared them the most; the bats chased their army; and the spiders chased their army!

There was a steady stream of injured people returning to town and each had another story to tell. Same old story; blood, guts, screaming, tears, crying; yet no death! Seems like forever since anyone has had something good to say!

Satan, sensing his followers were angry and bitter towards him, gathered all the wounded and sick people and asked them to be quiet. Then he spoke to them saying, "I know it seems like forever since there has been any peace, or joy, or love in our lives, but I have some good news to share with you. At least we're still alive and our bodies continue to support us! And we might find a place where we can see the sky again, and breathe fresh air and gaze at the stars!" And the people heard Satan and believed, and for the moment felt better.

A moment later, the terrible sound of screaming could be heard, and everyone knew the rest of the people were coming back, again. And they knew fear would be worse than before, and that it would seem to last forever, again.

As Satan heard the cries, he realized this place called Hell was his promised land! He realized he was a liar from the beginning and that he had no hope.

He wasn't a god and he feared what was coming against him. He saw the people look at him with hatred and anger and he was ashamed. He had deceived himself and every person he ever knew and he was alone. Worse than alone, everyone came against him in every way and he realized now he will be attacked forever by everyone in that kingdom; where death is, this place of great darkness; Hell.

And so this story goes on and on, and will forever. Satan, once great in Heaven, then cast out and became Prince of the Earth, now is and will always be nothing. No power, no glory, no hope, no love, no peace, no future, only darkness.

And it is going poorly for all who followed him there also! The thieves have nothing to steal, the drunkards have nothing to drink, the drug users have no drugs, the sexual perverts have no sexual satisfaction, the parents have no young children and the religious who never knew Jesus will never meet Him, and the rest who were too busy or thought they were doing well enough without God, well, now they know for sure they were sincerely wrong! And so it will be in Hell...forever!

ONE DAY

ONE DAY: When the fat lady sings,
When the wedding bell rings,
When the trumpet will sound,
When I'm caught-up; homeward bound,
There will be no more tears,
There will be no more fears,
There will be no more sorrow,
There will be no tomorrow,
We will walk in His light,
He will be our light,
We will eat from the tree,
He will set us all free,
We will give Him all praise,
He will show us His ways,
We will worship forever,
He will not leave us, ever,
There is no place to stumble,
There, all people are humble,
When nothing is sore,
ONE DAY: When time is no more.

Let me tell you more about this poem. At 5:00 a.m., I woke up from a dream I was having. And as I laid there thinking about this dream, I realized I should write a poem about it. So I got up; early for me; showered; and began writing, and this is what I saw.

There was an old man standing somewhere, looking intently somewhere at something. I said to the Lord; I can't write about this man and what he is seeing; I don't know what it is! So the Lord moved me to the man's view, and I could see.

I saw a bright place; really bright! There was movement, but I couldn't make out the faces; only shapes. I heard a blast from a trumpet, then more moving lights flashing by. A lady was singing in the background, and I heard wedding bells playing a new song, and it was good. I saw and heard these things, yet the rest was too beautiful to describe. I saw love, unity, and oneness, but couldn't define the picture. But I could feel the emotions that were there, so I wrote the rest of the poem describing verses from the Bible that best described what I was seeing. Then, at the last line of the poem, I saw the man standing there again; only as I blinked; he turned into a vapor like white mist, as he disappeared into the bright place, which was heaven. This poem then described this man's last moment of time. He was a Christian.

Now you picture your future. Can you see yourself standing somewhere, waiting for Jesus to welcome you home? I hope so, but if you're not sure, talk to God right now, while you have time. Remember the first line of this poem; it's not over till the fat lady sings! Or so the saying goes, but I add this thought. This moment comes like a thief in the night, like a blink of an eye; suddenly! So quickly that if you haven't received the Holy Spirit yet, you will never hear the fat lady sing! One moment here; one moment later there, but no time in between! Can you hear me now?

THE OTHER DAY

The Other Day............ When the darkness begins,
When there's judgment for sin,
When love disappears,
When we face all our fears,
There is no more delight,
There is no hope in sight,
There is no place to be,
There is no light to see,
We are trapped here in shame,
We have no one to blame,
We have anger and war,
We have nothing but sore,
We desire to leave,
We eternally grieve,
We have sorrow and pain,
We have tears but no reign,
There is no place to hide,
There is no other side,
When my screams took my voice,
The Other Day.............. When I still had a choice.

So, in the same way, this second poem was written. As soon as I finished writing about heaven, I realized this chapter was about hell. I prayed about how to write, but realized there was no dream about this place and being wise enough to know not to ask God for a nightmare, I simply put my thoughts in the guilty chair of God's judgment and began writing about the warnings in the Bible to those who reject the Holy Spirit right up to their death. So this poem describes the second death; the eternal place; separated from God.

So here's the bottom line. My thoughts were in the chair, but my body was still alive. I still had breath, so I still had a chance to be born again spiritually. But quickly, the last verse came, and I realize death had come for me, and I was shocked to realize I was in hell, and the last line of the poem came, and I was looking out at the other day, when I had a choice to make, and never made it! It was too late! My fears had come true, and it was too late to warn my friends about the indescribable horrors of being in darkness, alone, with screams of others; everywhere!

Boy, I'm glad this was just a poem! Or was it a warning for many who have not yet made peace with God? You decide where you're at; while you have time!

SLAVE TO SIN

Love me now, the way I am, the sinful man cried out,
Filthy words of anger, as his tongue began to shout.
Hidden in confusion, with no way to clear his head,
Sleepless nights and hopeless days; he knows who made his bed.

Give me just a little time, and space, to clear my foggy mind,
I can get it right this time; the world seems so unkind.
Don't judge me for the way I am; I know how things should be,
I'm doing pretty well, in fact; if only you could see!

So let me have a drink or two, to get me feeling right,
And let me smoke a little weed, before I work tonight.
And let me bet a buck or two; I need some extra dough,
And if I overdo it, well; who will ever know?

Seems like only yesterday, I set out to get straight,
Years of good intentions, set me back; I think it must be fate.
Still I'm gonna get it right; my bondage came so free,
I know I'm not a loser; someone must be cheating me!

Love me now; I'm sorry; did I cause you any pain?
It's hard to imagine a brighter day, while standing in the rain.
Remind me when I sober up; I want to make things right,
I need a better woman; maybe one that doesn't fight!

Give me just a little time; commitments not my style,
I know about depression; 'cause I've been there for a while.
And I know my health's an issue, and relationships are bad,
But at least I can remember, all the good times I once had!

So what then can I tell you; maybe someday I'll do right,
If only things were different; I would put up quite a fight.
I'm not saying that I'm quitting; I just want to wait and see,
Everything will be better; when I win the lottery!

Chapter 10
LET'S TALK ABOUT "IF"

"If" is used in the Bible over 1600 times! It is one of those conditional words we use to connect two thoughts or two actions together. There is often some measure of assumption implied, like, "if you do this, surely you will die". Or "if God says it, I believe it, because He cannot lie." Sometimes by using the word "if", we ask a question, yet leave room for doubt, or sometimes "if" asks us to make a decision. My point is simple: the word is short, but has the power to question your obedience, your faith or your motives. In God's Word, always watch for the "if", and think the verse through to make sure you understand what is being said, or asked or implied. I'll give examples.

In John 14:15, Jesus says, *"If you love me, you will obey what I command."*

In this verse, you are given a choice; you can love Him or not! But if you do love Him, you have no choice; you will obey His commands!

Let's look at another verse on the same subject.
In 2 John 1:6, it says, *"And this is love; that we walk in obedience to His commands. As you have heard from the beginning, His command is that you walk in love."*

This verse tells you what is love to God: that we obey what He says! No "if"! If you love; you obey! If you don't obey, you don't love God; you deceive yourself if you think any other way! If you truly believe that Jesus is the Truth, the Life, and the Way, your love for Him will reflect what you truly believe and do. Will you make poor choices? Yes. And He will discipline, and you will confess as sin, and repent of this sin, and He will forgive, and you will continue to follow Him. It is said that what a believer knows is what he or she talks about, but what a believer believes is how he or she lives their life. God's commands are not good ideas or options, they are to be applied to your life and obeyed!

Let's look at one more verse on the same subject.
Mark 12:30, Jesus says, *"Love the Lord your God with all your heart and with all your soul and with all your mind and with all your strength."*

Again, Jesus calls this verse His greatest command! Now look back to the "if" verse of John 14:15. Can you see now that "if" you believe in Jesus, and "if" you love Jesus, you must obey His commands! And if you do not truly love Him, you truly have a heart problem, and the love of Christ is not in you! Without His Spirit, your sin nature still lives, and somewhere along the way you deceived yourself or someone deceived you!

The only way to find out what went wrong is to pray and ask; get back into His word; and if you can, get sincere with God and truly make peace with Him!

In Mark 9, starting in verse 14, there is a story about a demon-possessed boy. The boy's father says to Jesus, verse 22, "*...But if you can do anything, take pity on us and help us.*" So here is the reply of Jesus in verse 23, "*'If you can?' Said Jesus. 'Everything is possible for him who believes.'*" And the father of the boy responded by saying, "*I do believe: help me overcome my unbelief!*" Jesus healed the boy.

So let's look at this verse again. The boy's father admitted that he had faith in Jesus, but he still had some measure of unbelief in his mind or heart. He knew who Jesus was, yet he said to Jesus "*If you can?*" Had this man known more about God and the power of the Holy Spirit and the power of Jesus' name, Jesus told the man his son could have been healed earlier; even through any person who believes.

In this case, even the disciples couldn't heal the boy, and in Mark 9:28-29, the disciples ask Jesus this, "*Why couldn't we drive out this demon?*" and Jesus replied, "*This kind of demon can come out only by prayer.*"

Now do you see why we spent so much time learning what "all kinds of prayer" are? Prayers are powerful; if you have His Spirit in you; and if you pray in Jesus name; and if it is God's will that healing comes during your prayer. If healing does not happen, or if your prayer request is not answered immediately, hold on to your faith, for most likely the timing of God's plans have not come yet. God may see the demon in the other person, but He is using their condition to grow your faith, or teach you something in your life through the possessed person! It's all about Jesus; His plans; His way; His timing; His purposes; for His glory! Study His word; seek His will; then do it!

Here is a thought I want to share with you. In Scripture, when the conditional word "if" is used, the statement made after it is a true statement, because God is holy, perfect, and because of His nature, He cannot and will not deceive. Therefore, you can assume that "if" you are not found doing or believing what the verse is saying, you are not included in the verse.

Let's look at another verse. In 2 Corinthians 5:17, it says, "*Therefore, if anyone is in Christ, he is a new Creation; the old has gone, the new has come!*"

Two things I want you to see here. One, when you hear or see the word "therefore", the verse you are about to read is true or conditional on the verses before this one. Secondly, the "if" is saying if you are a believer; if you have the Holy Spirit; if you are bearing good fruit; then you are a new creation in Christ! The old sin nature is defeated and gone! The

Holy Spirit changes you into a new person in Christ, you are born again spiritually in Christ; you belong to God and your body is a temple, and you must keep it Holy for Christ!

If you are not "in Christ", if you are not a new born again creation; if you are not producing good fruit; you are still "of the world"; you still are slave to sin; you are lost! And if you think there must be a mistake; you have deceived yourself!

Every time you read the word "if" in the Bible, stop and ask yourself "Am I doing what this verse says, or am I the one the verse is disqualifying?" You should be able to replace the word "if" with the word "I". I love; I obey; I believe; I trust; I worship; I understand God's Word; I praise God; I pray; I follow righteousness; I live for Christ; I am alive; I am free; I am forgiven; I am sealed; I am chosen; I am redeemed; I am saved; and I have eternal life; and heaven is my home; and I'm ready to go home! All these and more because of grace, as I placed my faith in Jesus; my Lord; my risen God; my Hope; my Salvation, my Shepherd; my Life! And if you are a born again follower of Jesus Christ, then find encouragement in this next verse.

> Hebrews 12:2-3, *"Let us fix our eyes on Jesus, the author and perfecter of our faith, who for the joy set before Him endured the cross, scorning its shame, and sat down at the right hand of the throne of God. Consider Him who endured such opposition from sinful men, so that you will not grow weary and lose heart."*

If this chapter spoke to your heart and you realize you never made peace with God, today can be your day of salvation.

1. If you believe there is a God and realize you are not Him...
2. If you realize you are a sinner and your sin separates you from God...
3. If you are ready to repent and ready to receive forgiveness...
4. If you believe in the Trinity of God and His word, the Bible...
5. If you are convinced that Jesus is Lord...
6. If you understand and can believe in the finished work of the cross...

Then you can confess these things through prayer to the Father, in the name of Jesus. Ask Him for forgiveness; ask to receive His forgiveness; tell Him you are ready to repent from sin. If you were sincere, God has now forgiven you, and you are now born again with His Spirit. You are now sealed until He redeems you! You have eternal life in Christ! You are now a slave to righteousness. To show your love for what He has done; read His word and obey what it says.

Now, so that the world and other believers know that you have been changed inside and are a new creation in Christ, go be baptized as an outward expression of your inward change.

Being righteous in God's eyes, your prayers are strong and powerful. Pray that God will lead you to a fellowship that will help you build a firm foundation in Christ. Don't wait too long to find this church, or Satan will attack you and rob you of your joy!

Pray that God will lead you into a Bible study group that will feed your spiritual hunger. Read the Bible every day and do what it says! You need mentorship and discipleship!

Pray that God will show you your spiritual gift or gifts, and pray He shows you what He wants you to do as ministry, and where He wants you to do it.

Pray that God will use you and your testimony to encourage others to come to know Jesus. The world's eyes are now on you.

Pray for more faith, wisdom, and perseverance. If you're not sure what to do and what not to do; do the opposite of what you have done all your life! Sin and righteousness have nothing in common!

Pray now for your unsaved family members, your friends, and your neighbors around you. Pray that they might be saved!

And now that your new life has begun, read the verses to come, so you may know for sure that your position in Christ is secure. The key words being "in Christ"! Be in His word; be in His will; be on His path and follow Him! Study His word; study His ways; then do what you have learned! Do as Jesus did; die to self; obey all His commands, not just the ones you choose! Listen to what His Spirit says and start today! Love God and give Him praise and all the glory! If you wait, Satan will keep you busy, and one disobedient week will turn into a month, and soon you will forget what God has done for you!

ETERNAL LIFE

1 John 5:13, *"I write these things to you who believe in the name of the Son of God so that you may know that you have eternal life."*

John 14:15-17, *"If you love Me, you will obey what I command. And I will ask the Father, and He will give you another Councilor to be with you forever, the Spirit of Truth."*

2 Corinthians 1:21-22, *"Now it is God who makes both us and you stand firm in Christ. He anointed us, set His seal of ownership on us, and put His Spirit in our hearts as a deposit, guaranteeing what is to come."*

Ephesians 1:13-14, *"And you also were included in Christ when you heard the word of truth, the gospel of your salvation. Having believed, you were marked in Him with a seal, the promised Holy Spirit, who is a deposit guaranteeing our inheritance until the redemption of those who are Gods possession; to the praise of His glory!"*

1 Corinthians 6:19-20, *"Do you not know that your body is a temple of the Holy Spirit, who is in you, whom you have received from God? You are not your own; you were bought at a price. Therefore, honor God with your body!"*

Romans 5:8-11, *"But God demonstrates His own love for us in this: While we were still sinners, Christ died for us. Since we have now been justified by His blood, how much more shall we be saved from God's wrath through Him! For if, when we were God's enemies, we were reconciled to Him through the death of His Son, how much more, having been reconciled, shall we be saved through His life! Not only is this so, but we now also rejoice in God through our Lord Jesus Christ, through whom we have now received reconciliation."*

And since God Himself has sealed those who were chosen; they are those who have believed in Him; those who love Him; those who obey Him; those whom the Father gave to His Son, and Jesus has lost none.

Revelation 5:5, *"Then one of the elders said to me, do not weep! See, the Lion of the Tribe of Judah, the Root of David, has triumphed. He is able to open the scroll and its seven seals."*

God sits on the throne in heaven, but Jesus is the only one in heaven or on earth or under the earth who is worthy to open God's seal!

Only Jesus saves, and He's coming back for His church! If you are thirsty ... come ... receive the water of life!

Romans 6:6, *"For we know that our old self was crucified with Him so that the body of sin might be done away with, that we should no longer be slaves to sin – because anyone who has died has been freed from sin."* Verse 8 – *"Now if we died with Christ, we believe that we will also live with Him."*

Romans 8:13, *"For if you live according to the sinful nature, you will die; but if you live by the Spirit, you put to death the misdeeds of the body, you will live, because those who are led by the Spirit of God are sons of God."*

1 John 2:15, *"Do not love the world or anything in the world."*

John 15:16, *"You did not choose Me, but I chose you, and appointed you to go and bear fruit that will last."*

Acts 1:10-11 says Jesus is coming back! Read about it!

"IF" – YOU CHOOSE

"If" is like the pivot point, which things are balanced on.
"If" is what you might receive, before the offer's gone.

"If" is a condition you will be in, whether you choose right or wrong.
"If" could be a measure of time, eternally short or eternally long.

"If" requires action, but the choice is up to you.
"If" will lead to action, if you take the time to do.

"If" will cause your mind to think, and may be hard to swallow.
"If" you do the thing it offers, it may be solid or hollow.

"If" will give you options, but it's not a word of blame.
"If" will make a difference, though conditions aren't the same.

"If" could lead to life or death; like together or separated.
"If" might lead to final breath; like Hell or elevated.

"If" could be the position you're in; like being left without.
"If" could be a wrong within; like being right about.

"If" your faith is tested; does it mean you will be detested?
"If" you choose to do right, will you never be arrested?

"If" you want to know the truth, can you still believe a lie?
"If" salvation comes not by works, does that mean you shouldn't try?

Yes the "If" in life has options, in the things we say and do,
No other "If" will save you, if you're thinking isn't true.

Jesus knows the "If" word, and He offers you a right,
"If" you choose Him as your savior, you receive eternal light.

FRIENDSHIP
A Short Story

There once were two young men who met each other at a local bar following a softball game. Sam played for a team that seemed to win all the time, especially when tournament time came around. Joe played first base for a team that struggled to field a full line-up from game to game. Not that they didn't have talent, they just weren't committed to winning. Funny how players on the field can be so different, and yet, after the game, they go to the same places, enjoy the same things, and basically, have most things in common.

And so it was with Sam and Joe. The more time they spent together, the more they realized how much they enjoyed hanging out together. To keep this story short, let me give you an idea of who these young men were, and how their friendship grew.

Sam was 23 when he met Joe. Married; two kids; small house. His wife, Sue, was 21, attractive, liked to do everything Sam did, and seemed to hold her own at whatever she applied herself to. Sam worked at a local hardware store and enjoyed his job. If all went well, he hoped to one day own his own store and perhaps retire at a younger than 65 age so he and Sue could travel and enjoy their health as long as they could.

Joe was 24 when he met Sam. Married; two kids; small house. His wife, Jill, was a good cook, enjoyed company on weekends, and was up to doing whatever anyone else wanted to do. In short, just fun to be around. Joe worked at McDonalds his junior and senior years of high school, and after graduation, got hired as a cook at a small restaurant close to home. Not much hope for wage advancement, but he liked cooking and made enough to pay the bills. Most guys teased Joe for being so laid back and care free, but Joe didn't care; life was good.

So there you have it. Two ordinary men forming a friendship that would eventually last a lifetime. So much in common; wives, family, young, care free. And as time went on, they even found more things they enjoyed together, which included bowling, camping, fishing, and snowmobiling. They even bought 4 wheelers together so they could enjoy hunting trips when they could find the time; again, life was good!

Now remember, this is a short story, so we have to make a jump forward a few years! Let's pick the story up at their 15th class reunion. Both Joe and Sam have been divorced for a few years by now. Jill left Joe two years ago when she found out about an affair Joe was having with a waitress at the restaurant. Sue divorced Sam four years ago when she found out that the bar waitress at their favorite pub gave birth to Sam's third child! Shortly after their divorce, Sam married the bar maid, Wanda. Turns out she wasn't a nice girl; they got divorced before their 2nd anniversary. Anyway, Sam and Joe are still friends and find themselves at a table at their 15th reunion. Drinks are flowing, everyone is silly happy, when a strange conversation developed. One of the men at the table, Bill, looked over to Sam, and asked him a question. Keep in mind that Bill was class President, captain of the basketball team, and homecoming King in football. Bill was smart! Valedictorian of their class! Bills parents were self-made millionaires in real estate and gave Bill a million dollars for his graduation gift! This same Bill turned to Sam and asked "Is anyone in this room really happy? Do we have to get drunk to smile? Is there any meaning to life other than get what you can get and then die? Do I have, or do you have a purpose in all this?" Bill added: "If you can answer any of these questions, please do! My life is so miserable I wish I was never born!"

Wow! This was Bill crying out to us! Bill, the only one we thought had everything all together! Bill, the EF Hutton of the class, who when he spoke, everyone listened. In fact, you could hear a pin drop at our table! We were all in shock! Who would ask such questions anyway, especially Bill, the one everyone had set up high on our pedestals! And so it was that evening; silence; sadness; confusion! Truth is, not one of us had any answers to Bill's questions. We sat in silence for about a half an hour, though it seemed hours! When finally, someone broke the ice by saying – "Hey –good questions; let's get drunk." And we did.

From time to time, we reminded each other of that night and remember the questions Bill had voiced. Mostly we remember how Bill got in a car wreck on his way home that evening and died. I remember thinking what a bummer it was for Bill to die with so many unanswered questions. As I ponder, little did I know that one day I would have answers, and I can't help from wondering if lives would have been changed if I had learned more about life myself at an earlier age. Oh well, can't go back. Let's take another jump in time!

Here we are, getting closer to 50 now! Sam and Joe are still best friends. Sam's on his third wife and Joe's on his second. Both have settled down, or should I say, slowed down! Anyway, they still have toys, but they don't get used much anymore. They still like a drink now and then, but usually at home. Older and wiser, yep, that's what their getting! No more drunken parties, no more messing around with women; just work, wives and sleep. Becoming wiser and more comfortable every year! Sam's boss retired last year and sold him the hardware store at a great price. Sam also negotiated his boss' house into the deal, so overnight, Sam completed his youthful dream of owning his own store and one day moving into a big, nice house. Sam was content at last.

Joe was doing well too! Thirty years of service at the same restaurant, and now is retiring early with enough pension to draw until social security kicks in. Joe's wife, Beth, inherited a nice home just down the street from Sam's new house when her parents died. She also received a nice settlement when her first husband died of cancer at the young age of 58. At least for now, life is good!

So, one more jump in time and I'll wind up this story. Five years later. Same town, same friends, all living the American dream; finally! Grandchildren and great grandchildren take up most of the days.

Sam has the opportunity to sell the store at a sweet profit, and decides to do so. Joe and Beth continue to live a good retirement age life, and still enjoy kids, camping, and an occasional movie.

About a year ago, something changed. Sam and his wife invited Joe and Beth over to the house for a barbeque. At the dinner table, small talk led into a deeper subject when Joe asked, "Hey, remember Bill and the last time we saw him? Remember all the questions he had that night? What a night!"

Once again, though many years later, the same blank look came over both Sam and Joe. With empty hearts, a tear came out of both of them! Beth and Sam's wife sensed their sorrow, and became sober also. After a time of silence, Sam spoke up, saying, "We better look deeper into these matters and find out what we've been missing all these years!" All agreed, and at least for the moment, all was good.

The next day, Joe walked over to Sam's house and together they moved to the den, where Sam had his office desk in the corner of the room. They went to the computer and began a word search. They talked it over, trying to remember the key words to their old friend Bill's questions. Sam entered: truth, life, purpose and waited to see what the internet might have to say about these things. To their amazement, pages of information came up! After reading many, they noticed several referred to God. Some offered Bible verses, some offered books to read, and some offered answers to life's questions. For some reason, they both agreed to start with God, since neither knew anything about Him.

That click cost Sam his life! God, Bible verses, new teachings, unlimited information, with answers to every question they could think of! Day after day for nearly a month, Sam and Joe read. Neither could explain how so much information was out there that they never knew even existed!

This was exciting stuff! While discussing these things with their wives, all agreed it was time to visit a church. Not knowing where to start, they decided to attend a small Baptist church only 3 miles away. Being small, if they didn't like it, they could slip out the back door unnoticed. Sunday came. They walked in and took the first available pew and sat down. So far, so good. The preacher greeted everyone and after a few songs, the message began. "God bless you! He has a purpose and a plan for your life. He sent His Son to die on the cross to pay the penalty for sin. Jesus shed His blood for you so that you may live. Jesus died for your sins and the sins of all the world. Jesus was buried; Jesus rose again and conquered death; Jesus ministered to His disciples, and then ascended into heaven. Jesus is coming back to gather His people; those who love Him. Jesus sent His Holy Spirit to earth to be with all who would believe in Him and receive Him as Lord. Jesus waits for you to repent and seek Him."

The message continued, "Are you willing to repent? Are you ready to confess your sins and ask for forgiveness? Are you ready to receive your free gift of salvation? Are you ready to put your faith and trust into the person of Jesus Christ, Lord of lords, King of kings? If so, come forward now and pray with me."

The music began to play. People began to sing a hymn. A young couple walked forward and began talking to the Pastor. Sam's heart was pounding. He felt led to go forward. As Sam stood up, his wife grabbed his arm to join him. God was calling and Sam heard and answered. They walked forward. In an awkward moment, Joe and Beth joined them up front. Music was playing, prayers were said and prayer was heard. Lives were changed. For now, all was well!

Sam and Joe were closer now than ever before. Sam and his wife sold their house and went to the mission field in Africa. Joe and Beth became members of the Baptist church, and Joe became a part of the prayer team, and would become a Sunday school teacher of the 5 to 6 year olds. Beth joined the choir, and sometimes worked in the nursery.

One day, while Sam and his wife were home on furlough, Joe and Beth joined them for supper at their favorite local restaurant. The same place where Joe had worked for 30 years, and many friends were still around to greet them as they walked in the door. What a night! Steak and shrimp, salad bar, glass of wine, best of friends with stories of an awesome God.

At the table next to them sat four well dressed men. Quiet; polite; also enjoying the evening. While overhearing Sam's praises of how God was working in Africa, one of the men leaned over and asked Sam if he meant to say Allah? Sam said no, God. The man asked Sam if he believed in Jesus also. Sam responded "Yes, God the Father, God the Son, and God the Holy Spirit. Jesus is the Son. One God, revealed to us as three persons. Do you understand this teaching of the Trinity?"

The man paused for a moment, looked at the other three at his table, then stared directly at Sam and without warning, guns were drawn; shots were fired. Eight people died that night, including Sam, Joe, their wives, two waitresses, one cook, and a man coming in the front door at the wrong time. The four shooters were caught, tried, and sentenced to life in prison. Almost the end of this story.

Me? I've been around, and have known Sam and Joe most of my life. I graduated in the same class, played sports with them. I shared many hunting stories with them, and went to their weddings. I was at the table the night Bill died. I was in church the day Sam and Joe went forward, and I was sitting at the table next to Sam when he was shot to death by those men. I went to their funeral, and I miss them.

I saw Sam one more time, in a vision, talking to Jesus. They were in heaven, and Sam asked Jesus "I've been looking for my friend Joe and can't find him." Jesus responded; I saw you with that person many times during your lifetime, but I never knew him."

As Sam walked away, Jesus spoke to him in a gentle voice "Are you going to miss Joe?" Sam turned around, smiled, and said "Joe who?"

> Matthew 7:21-23, *"Not everyone who says to Me, Lord, Lord, will enter the kingdom of heaven. But only he who does the will of My Father who is in heaven. Many will say to Me on that day, 'Lord, Lord, did we not prophesy in Your name, and in Your name drive out demons and perform many miracles?' Then I will tell them plainly, I never knew you. Away from Me, you evildoers!"*

> Revelation 21:4, *"He will wipe away every tear from their eyes. There will be no more death or mourning or crying or pain, for the old order of things has passed away."*

Sam was a good and loyal friend to Joe, but when Jesus called him, Sam heard and did what Jesus said to do. First, receive Him, and then, obey Him. Joe was a nice guy and also a loyal friend. He went forward in church because Sam did, and though he prayed a prayer and saw his life changing, God was not his Lord. He did good things because he wanted to be a nice guy, but he never heard God's voice and never did God's will. Joe missed the love relationship that Jesus wanted.

When Jesus told Sam "I never knew him", Sam understood. It is good to know God and Jesus and the Holy Spirit. It is infinitely better for you if THEY know you!

BELIEVER TO UNBELIEVER

If the truth I speak might hurt you, would you rather hear a lie,
Should we stop communication, if we don't see eye to eye.
Is a weakness worth revealing, is the truth so hard to take,
Can a heart become so bitter, that it can't admit mistake.

If I take the time to teach you, will you take the time to care,
Even if you should reject me; I'm not going anywhere!
There is so much good in giving; it's so sad when love is blind,
Life is hard enough just living, you don't have to be unkind.

Test me, if you're willing, you will find I am sincere,
Bring out, into the open, what it is that isn't clear.
I will share what I am learning, but you have to want to change,
I can organize the present, but let's not just rearrange.

I am offering my friendship; I am offering my heart,
I don't ask for any payment; I just ask when I can start!
I can't change the things that hurt you, and I won't give them a name,
I would rather change your future, than to designate the blame.

JOY IN SERVING

Jesus; You gave me the strength to be good,
Now, wouldn't it be nice, if the world understood!
I get so excited; I jump up and shout!
Then, sadly remember; the lost live without.
So fill me with wisdom, put truth in my heart,
Turn loose my emotions, show where I should start.
I know you can use me, please show me the way,
Some say there's no hurry, but I say "TODAY"!
I'm learning and teaching, I'm sharing Your joy,
My arms are wide open, Your word, I employ.
Now send me Your children, I'll plant a good seed,
Then You, caring Father, can provide all they need.
And when they have Spirit, our family will grow,
I love seeing faces, when Your light starts to glow!
For me, comes assurance, I'm doing God's will,
A warm sweet contentment, only Jesus can fulfill.

Chapter 11
SCRIPTURES THAT CHALLENGE THE SOUL

Matthew 7:13-14 says, *"Enter through the narrow gate, for wide is the gate and broad is the road that leads to destruction, and many enter through it. But small is the gate and narrow the road that leads to life, and only a few find it."*

The Bible often refers to believers as His sheep.

And in John 10:7, Jesus said, *"I tell you the truth, I am the gate for the sheep: whoever enters through Me will be saved."*

And in verse 9, Jesus repeats, *"I am the gate; whoever enters through Me will be saved."*

In this generation, we are a tolerant people. If there are twenty churches in your town, everyone wants to believe that it is their church that preaches and teaches the truth. And it is their teaching that is sound. It's like saying, since there is only one God, all roads must lead to Him. And since God is love, all people who say they love God must be going to heaven.

The problem with this thinking is that the Bible was a gift from God, and it reveals the truth, and Jesus is the Truth, and He says He is the only way to heaven. Not by works, so that no man may boast of what he has done to deserve God's favor.

God's love is awesome, and He gives it freely and unconditionally. It was God who sent His Son to die on the cross. Jesus knew He was born on earth to die for the sins of the world, and His love for the Father was shown perfectly through His obedience unto death. Yes, God is love. But equally true is that God is just, and both must balance perfectly.

Jesus said, "I will judge all the sins of the world". Jesus said we believers should obey Him, and He will make all things right. He will punish those who reject Him, and also those who reject His followers. Justice will be perfect because God knows every thought, deed, motivation, circumstance and condition of every heart involved in every sin ever committed!

God had a plan before He created the heavens and the earth. He spoke into existence all that has been made; He gave life to mankind; and He is STILL in control today. He put His will into motion and did what needed to be done to make peace with whosoever calls upon His Name. The message of the cross has been accomplished, and the penalty for sin has been paid; God's love has been revealed; now hear the rest of the story and choose Jesus as you Lord and Savior.

God's love has been shown: in His creation; in His mercy; in His grace; in His faithfulness; in the finished work of the cross; in His Son; through His Spirit; in His offer for eternal life.

Not all people will be saved from judgment, but only those who come to love Jesus and receive His Spirit and obey the commands He has gracefully given.

> Matthew 7:21-27, Jesus says, *"Not everyone who says to Me, "Lord, Lord" will enter the kingdom of heaven, but only he who does the will of My Father who is in heaven. Many will say to Me on judgment day, 'Lord, Lord, did we not prophesy in Your name, and in Your name drive out demons and perform miracles?' Then I will tell them plainly, 'I never knew you. Away from Me, you evildoers!' Therefore, everyone who hears these words of Mine and puts them into practice is like a wise man who built his house on the rock. The rain came down, the streams rose, and the winds blew and beat against that house, yet it did not fall, because it had its foundation on the rock. But everyone who hears these words of Mine and does not put them into practice is like a foolish man who built his house on sand. The rain came down, the streams rose, and the winds blew and beat against that house, and it fell with a great crash."*

WOW! This warning challenges our thinking and our heart! This warning is written to make us aware that it is not enough to "say" we are Christians, we must prove our love to God through our obedience to His word. But to this, we must have sincere motives. And to this, we must do God's will, not our own; God's way, not what we would rather do; God's timing, not when we feel like doing it or if we feel like doing it; with an attitude of gratitude for choosing us, and all these things for God's glory, not ours. God doesn't want us to impress Him with good works that we choose to do. Rather, He wants to do His will through us, as He accomplishes those things He has planned, for whatever purpose He is in the process of accomplishing. Because only God is good, we who are being used by God say all the time, 'Not me, but Christ in me has done these good things." I take no credit for what He has done, or what He is doing, or what He will accomplish in the future. I simply praise Him for what He has done, and trust in Him for all things.

> To the religious person who wants to add "good works" to gain their salvation, the Bible has this to say in Isaiah 64:6, *"All of us have become like one who is unclean, and all our righteous acts are like filthy rags; we all shrivel up like a leaf, and like the wind, our sins sweep us away."*

This verse is saying that even our best efforts are still infected with sin. If we receive Christ as Lord and receive His Holy Spirit into our hearts, we are cleansed by HIS righteousness. But many are deceived into thinking their works will help save them from God's judgment, but Scripture doesn't say that! Not by works so that NO MAN may boast of what he has done to deserve the free gift of eternal life.

It is not enough that we know Jesus; but ask the question, "Does He know ME?" Many times in Scripture, we are warned not to deceive ourselves or not to be deceived by others. Is your faith in God ALONE, or have you added something to His word to make you feel better about yourself? In our close personal love relationship with God, our desire is to become more like Jesus. This takes commitment to His word; reading, believing, and doing the commands the Bible tells us to do. Are you attending a healthy church? Are you active in obedience and in ministry? Do you enjoy giving of your tithes, gifts and offerings? Do you pray all kinds of prayers and read the Bible daily? Every moment you fail to do these things you are ignoring God and His will for your life!

In this verse, Matthew declares people doing religious activity as "evil doers". Therefore, how much worse off are those who do even less? Purify your hearts while you have time, for no one is promised tomorrow! For with God, all things are possible!

> Matthew 12:46-48, Jesus describes His true family saying, *"While Jesus was still talking to the crowd His mother and brothers stood outside, wanting to speak to Him. Someone told Him, 'Your mother and brothers are standing outside, wanting to speak to You.' Jesus replied to him, 'Who is My mother, and who are My brothers?' Pointing to His disciples, He said, 'Here are My mother and My brothers, for whoever does the will of My Father in heaven is My brother and sister and mother.'"*

Jesus is not saying that His earthly family is to be ignored or not valued. Jesus is talking about a spiritual relationship with God the Father which builds the body of Christ, and Jesus is the Head of that body. And as believers in Christ, our spiritual brothers and sisters are those who are equally yoked to Christ.

Jesus teaches us as believers to love our spouses and our children, and to honor our fathers and mothers, but Jesus makes it clear that God must come first! Jesus knew who was standing at the door, but He wanted to make it clear that He was from God above, and His priorities were doing God's will, not the will of an earthly mother or earthly brother.

Some people call their Pastor or under-shepherd "Father", but this is disobedience to God.

Jesus said in Matthew 23:9, *"And do not call anyone on earth father, for you have one Father, and He is in heaven."*

In your home, call your dad – Dad or Daddy or Pop or Papa! In your church, don't give the man preaching deity he does not deserve! Call him preacher, messenger, brother, Pastor or by his earthly name.

2 Corinthians 6:14-18 says, *"Do not be yoked together with unbelievers. For what do righteousness and wickedness have in common? Or what fellowship can light have with darkness? What harmony is there between Christ and Satan? What does a believer have in common with an unbeliever? What agreement is there between the Temple of God and idols? For we are the temple of the living God. And God has said, 'I will live with them and walk among them, and I will be their God, and they will be my people. Therefore come out from them and be separate,' says the Lord. 'Touch no unclean thing and I will receive you. I will be a Father to you, and you will be my sons and daughters,' says the Lord Almighty."*

Non-believers; those who are spiritually dead; those who live in darkness; those who live under the authority of Satan and his demons; those who are not born again; those who are condemned already and are dying to go to hell; this Scripture has no warning for you! In your sin nature, you cannot understand this warning!

But to you who have been set apart by God; you who have received the Holy Spirit; you who love God; you who have hope of eternal life; you whom God chose to do His will; you, the body of Christ; you who have the power and strength to resist the devil and his lies; it is you who are warned to obey His commands!

"Do not" is a command which means if you love God, you will obey. If you disobey, you will be disciplined by God. If you refuse to obey after discipline, your heart condition may reveal that you really don't love God after all! If that was true, the second verses we discussed, Matthew 7:21-27, will reveal the true condition of your soul.

This warning and command is challenging, but can be understood. And with God's help, relationships can be honoring to God. The believer, who is looking for a partner, looks for another believer for marriage. Non-believers have no loyalty to God; no commitment, standards or integrity to represent. Believers should not compromise their faith. What the world declares as acceptable is often sin and rebellion towards God. Those who compromise God's trust will be punished.

So, how can we as believers work out this conflict? Easier than it sounds, if we trust that God will work all things for good for those who love Him. We are called to be in the world but not "of the world". We go forward in love, teaching, preaching and declaring God's Word and His gospel. We encourage, we pray for, and we stay in contact, but we spend our intimate time with God and His followers. We love our families and friends, and help them in every way we can. If they reject us, they are rejecting Jesus, and by rejecting Jesus, they reject Father God because they are one.

It is God's hope that all would be saved and come to repentance. Therefore, that becomes my hope and the hope of all believers. We stand firm, obeying God's Word, because we know it is true, and since only Jesus saves, we have faith that God's grace is sufficient, and that He will reward all those who earnestly seek Him. So we pray and trust in Jesus to work out all things.

Have we sinned against God in our relationships? I believe we all have. But when we realize what we have done, we go to God in prayer, and we confess what has happened.

> 1 John 1:9 says, *"If we confess our sins, He is faithful and just and will forgive us our sins and purify us from all unrighteousness."*

This is not a salvation prayer. We did that when we settled our position in Christ and received His Holy Spirit that sealed us until redemption. This is a relationship prayer, restoring our fellowship with God and keeping our joy in Christ alive.

> Matthew 10:34-39, Jesus says, *"Do not suppose that I have come to bring peace to the earth. I did not come to make peace, but a sword. For I have come to turn a man against his father, a daughter against her mother, a daughter-in-law against her mother-in-law; a man's enemies will be the members of his own household. Anyone who loves his father or mother more than Me is not worthy of Me. Anyone who does not take his cross and follow Me is not worthy of Me. Whoever finds his life will lose it, and whoever loses his life for My sake will find it."*

If God was only love, and justice was not a part of His perfect nature, everyone born on earth, spiritually dead, would be saved and have eternal life in heaven. Words like "judgment", "if", "punishment" and "thou shall" would be taken out of the Bible, because they would have no value to God's purposes or God's plans.

If God was only justice, and love was not a part of His perfect nature, everyone born on earth would end up in hell. For all have sinned, no one seeks God, no one is righteous, God's love would not be known, and Jesus wouldn't have gone to the cross; for we would all get what we deserve, which is eternal death.

But God is love, and God is just, and God is perfect in all that He does. His love and justice are perfectly equal, and His judgments, based on His knowledge and wisdom, are always perfectly made. He knows your heart; He knows your motives; He knows ALL THINGS! Therefore, you can trust that God will reward you perfectly according to your lifetime of choices, and your lifetime of beliefs, and your final decision to accept or reject Jesus as Lord. When your life on earth is over, you will appear in God's court, and your eternal destination will be revealed. Heaven waits for those who believed in Jesus, which was God's plan. Hell waits for those who made their own plans; lived their own life; trusted in themselves and the world; and were deceived.

We know these things are true, because the Bible told us so, and we believe. So the "sting" or "surprise" in these Matthew 10 verses is not shocking to us; they simply prepare us for what is to come. It is God's hope that all would be saved and be spared eternal death, but if He willed it upon your life, you would have no choice or say in the matter, and God loves us so deeply, He accepts your choice, and will reward you justly.

To choose Christ over all choices brings glory to God. To belong to Christ, to obey Christ; to follow Christ; to become more like Christ, that is to honor Him; and true believers are honored to be a part of His body.

Just as Jesus died on the cross as an example of true love towards God and humanity; we who come to believe in Jesus and receive Him as Lord, we also receive His love. And this love is not only for us, but is for others to receive through us. We who know God must learn to die to our self desires; giving up our plans for success for the good of God's plans and His purposes. So for the greater good of our God, we allow Him to move us to places He wants to use us. He chooses where I live; where I work; where I travel; when I travel; for His glory. What I might have had or what I might have accomplished means nothing compared to what I do have in Christ today.

> 2 Timothy 3:1-5 says, *"But mark this: There will be terrible times in the last days. People will be lovers of themselves, lovers of money, boastful, proud, abusive, disobedient to their parents, ungrateful, unholy, without love, unforgiving, slanderous, without self control, brutal, not lovers of the good, treacherous, rash, conceited, lovers of pleasure rather than lovers of God, having a form of godliness but denying its power. Have nothing to do with them.*

These verses have four valuable warnings written in them. One, all people will sense when the world is nearing the end when you see people doing all the things on this list at the same time. To the believer, it gives us peace knowing Jesus will return soon for His church.

The second warning is obvious. If you read this list and you can see yourself taking part of any of these things, you know the time has come to repent and get off the list while you still can! The third warning is to the religious, who think they are doing okay, but are not living according to the Spirit.

> In Galatians 5:22-25, God says, *"But the fruit of the Spirit is love, joy, peace, patience, kindness, goodness, faithfulness, gentleness and self control. Those who belong to Christ Jesus have crucified the sinful nature with its passions and desires. Since we live by the Spirit, let us keep in step with the Spirit."*

If God is working in us and through us, what He produces is good fruit; and we who are seen will appear fruitful and different from others in a good way. Since the Bible says a good tree produces good fruit, and that a bad tree cannot; the warning is how are you doing? If you say you love God, do everything you can to please Him, thus proving your love to others.

> In Galatians 6:7-8 God's Word says, *"Do not be deceived; God cannot be mocked. A man reaps what he sows. The one who sows to please his sinful nature, from that nature will reap destruction. The one who sows to please the Spirit, from the Spirit will reap eternal life."*

A friend and Pastor once told me this: When you walk into McDonald's, you don't turn into a hamburger. In the same way, by walking into a church, you don't turn into a Christian. One name: Jesus; one way: Jesus is that way; one door: and Jesus is that door; one gate: and Jesus is that gate.

> Romans 10:17 says, *"Faith comes from hearing the message, and the message is heard through the word of Christ."*

Are you reading the Bible and living your life as if the stories in it are describing you?

And then, the fourth warning. Have nothing to do with the people on this warning list! Minister to them and encourage them to seek and know the truth, but don't do the things they do as non-believers, or you may find out that your heart's desire is to be like those on the list, rather than to desire to be like Christ! In which case you would reveal the true condition of your heart, which in itself reveals you've been deceived.

> 1 Corinthians 6:9-10 says, *"Do you not know that the wicked will not inherit the kingdom of God? Do not be deceived; neither the sexually immoral nor idolaters nor adulterers nor male prostitutes nor homosexual offenders nor thieves nor the greedy nor drunkards nor slanderers nor swindlers will inherit the kingdom of God."*

Another list, another warning: Don't be deceived! As the end times approach, evil people, evil spirits and wicked sinners will come into the open and proudly declare their independence of God's ways. People will be tolerant of all sinful behavior. Watching as two dogs in heat come together will seem more natural than the queer behavior between people. Thieves will take from others what they want, and yet be mad at the lawmakers when they get caught. Greed will cause even peaceful people to over spend and buy things they can't afford. People will be guilty until proven innocent. More decisions will be made under the influence of drugs and alcohol than decisions made for Christ. And many people will blame God for not blessing them!

Can you imagine our government when we elect people to represent the majority of our country? To stay in office, they have to represent "We, the people"! Will government prosper, or steal from this fund to pay that fund? Will they represent God's values or reflect the condition of the people who voted them into office?

God has answers that even governments don't consider. God loves us, but we ignore Him. God will offer us all forgiveness, but we are too proud to ask. God shows us the way, but we are too busy to find it. God sees all our needs, but we only see what we want. God offers us a picture of hope and life; you hold the camera; take the picture!

> Galatians 5:19 says, *"The acts of the sinful nature are obvious: sexual immorality, impurity, and debauchery, idolatry, witchcraft, hatred, discord, jealousy, fits of rage, selfish ambition, dissensions, factions, envy, drunkenness, orgies, and the like. I warn you, as I did before, that those who live like this will not inherit the kingdom of God."*

Another list, warning those who hold on to their sin nature and follow the ways of the world. Satan and his followers have heard God's Word and do anything they can to corrupt it. To be a follower of the devil, all you have to do is not become a born again follower of Jesus Christ. We are all born spiritually dead already, and will remain separated from God in this world and in the future to come. Eternal: yes; but not life: death.

As in God's other warning lists, you can imagine how many people are still on this list! Wide is the road to hell and many follow it! If you know anyone who may live this way, I encourage you to talk to them and give them hope for the future!

Like all of God's warnings, there remains only one way to get off the lists: identify your need to be saved. Discover that there is a God and you are not Him! Read His word; seek His truth; believe His story and receive Jesus as Lord. Confess what you learn to be wrong; ask for forgiveness; receive the Holy Spirit and begin your new life in Christ. Join a church; study His word; do His word; share your faith; live for God.

James says in James 4:4, *"You adulterous people, don't you know that friendship with the world is hatred toward God? Anyone who chooses to be a friend of the world becomes an enemy of God."*

Just another warning reminding us to protect our hearts, eyes, and ears from the things the worldly people do without conviction or regret. Christians are to be "in" the world but not "of" the world. There are many things that unchurched people do that don't break the written laws of the land, yet break the commandments of God. As people become more and more immoral, even the moral code of ethics is corrupted to the point of extinction. When sexual perversions and adultery become so common that there is no resistance towards it, our society is reduced to garbage. And like real garbage, our lifestyles begin to stink and become an abomination to God. And at the same time, we call our nation a Christian nation and stamp our money with "IN GOD WE TRUST"!

In Luke 11:23, Jesus says, *"He who is not with Me is against Me, and he who does not gather with Me, scatters."*

In a world that wants to win at all cost, isn't it amazing that people follow the devil, even though God will defeat him and all of his followers, and cast them into HELL! Choose life in Jesus and win eternal joy, or choose death with Satan and be punished forever in hell! Yes, I was 46 when I became a believer; I was blind, but now see! Don't spend another moment in darkness. Ask God to turn on your light so you can see!

James 1:22 says, *"Do not merely listen to the word, and so deceive yourselves. Do what it says."*

To hear God's Word and ignore it is worse that never hearing it! Once you know what the right way to live and behave is, you will have no excuse when judgment comes. God tells you what to do to make peace with Him, and most ignore His attempts to enlighten them. Reasons only explain why you chose not to do something. Excuses release you from a penalty. The penalty for sinful behavior is death, and the only person in the world who could pay the price was Jesus. A sinless man who took upon Himself the sins of the world to satisfy God's justice. When we believe in Him; He pays our death sentence for us, and we become His. Jesus, the Judge, has pardoned our sins because He paid the penalty for our sins. There is no excuse available other than what Jesus has done! If you believe any lie, you have been deceived. Reasons don't excuse the guilty of the sin verdict!

A SHORT STORY

The other night while I was sleeping, I suddenly awoke to a bright light, and I was startled; though not afraid. At first, I thought I was standing at a narrow gate, but then realized the light was for me, and I entered into the light. At that very moment, the Light spoke to me, saying, "Welcome, my good and faithful servant." Again, at that very moment, I realized that the Light who spoke to me before; which I had heard in days past, was Jesus.

In my moment of astonishment, I realized my eyes were still closed from the blinding brightness of the Light. Just as I started to open my eyes, the voice spoke again. He asked, "Before I open your eyes to My Kingdom, is there any requests you may have of Me?" I thought for a moment, and then asked if I could look back into the darkness and see my family and friends one last time. Knowing that their time had not yet come, Jesus granted my request, yet also gave me this instruction. I have given you eyes to see, and when you have seen enough, you will have peace in your soul. And when you are ready, come to Me, and I will give you a tour of My Kingdom and your home.

I understood. I stood at the edge of darkness in amazement. As I looked to the left and right, the barrier was like a wall, yet I couldn't touch it. When I tried, the darkness was exposed and I could not feel it, yet the darkness could not reach me in any way. The darkness wanted to, but it had no power in itself. Then I realized that time was moving in the darkness, yet it was still where I was standing. Then I remembered that Scripture spoke about eternal things and temporary things, and that time was one of those things.

Again, I looked into the darkness, and looked for my family and friends. Below me were small beams of light, like hundreds of speeding cars on many huge freeways, all traveling through time at a quick pace. I couldn't see where everyone was going, but I remember watching and wondering who they were. Every once in a while, I saw people coming up our hill, on a straight and narrow path, then they would disappear into the same gate I once arrived at.

I discovered that if I concentrated and focused hard enough, I could see the lives of the people who had once been close to me. I saw my church friend. It took me a while, but I figured out eventually that days, weeks and years were going by before my eyes. Weird! Anyway, I focused on my church friend. He went to church, but other than that, not many changes. It was then when I realized I could see two things, good fruit that pleased God and sin that didn't please God. It didn't take long to realize my church friend had no fruit, and I was worried. Then more that worried when I saw him driving down the wide freeway towards the end. And then I saw down the road, the sign "destruction", and my friend disappeared. I never saw him again.

I looked back into the world, and saw more of my friends. I expected to see happy faces,
laughter, and people having fun. But I was wrong! I saw what God sees all the time, people in a hurry to go nowhere. People working 60 hours a week to make money, so they could buy more stuff. Tired people, sick people who had stuff but didn't have time to use it all, because they were tired, sick, or resting so they could go to work again. I saw a few with good works in their hearts, and one by one they came to the narrow path that led to the gate of Light. All the rest eventually drove the freeway towards destruction and disappeared.

I watched for a long time, then turned away and walked into the Light again. I never looked back.

Chapter 12
UNCOMPREHENSIBLE TRUTHS: MYSTERIES

In the New Testament of the Bible, there are 27 verses referring to mysteries. If Scripture at times has verses that seem to contradict; and it does; we know this: God's Word is perfect and complete without error, so when these moments come, we know it is our understanding that is incomplete. And concerning these mysteries, it is grace that will allow us to move forward, and by faith, we believe God will reveal all truths to us at the proper time; often I believe when we reach heaven! Until then; we live our lives loving God and showing His love to others.

Though the Bible is truth and written accurately, when men use their own understandings to relay what God is saying, sometimes there is a difference of opinion; or should I say usually! Never-the-less, the Bible also says that believers hear God and that they know what He is saying to them. When God speaks to a believer; the believer obeys. If you are confused when God speaks, maybe it's NOT God! Until you're sure, pray for guidance, understanding and wisdom. Obey God's Word to the best of your understanding, and trust that God will use you and work out all things for good to those who love Him.

Jesus often spoke in parables, which are stories in which He used familiar teachings, things or objects which people understood, yet the purpose of the story was to reveal a spiritual truth. In order to understand the story, you have to think it through. The truth of the story would be hidden from those who were too stubborn or prejudiced to hear the teaching.

> In Mark 4:11 Jesus says, *"The secret of the kingdom of God has been given to you. But to those on the outside everything is said in parables so that they may be ever seeing but never perceiving, and ever hearing but never understanding; otherwise they might turn and be forgiven."*

This parable explanation was given to the 12 disciples who asked Jesus to explain the meaning. The actual parable of the sower was preached to many who had gathered to hear Jesus speak (Mark 4:1-9).

Let's look closer into Scripture and see if we can identify spiritual teachings. First, it says, "The kingdom of God is a secret." Until Jesus explained the story, even His disciples didn't understand. Jesus chose His disciples; they did not choose Him; yet they chose to follow when they were told to do so.

But now look at the next sentence. To "those on the outside" STOP! Is there an "in crowd" and a "not in the in crowd"? Does God give some ears to hear and eyes to see, and to some ears and eyes that do not? Does God harden hearts or do prideful people harden their own? Was God using His sovereignty to choose a few, or was He using His foreknowledge to see that most would not be able to respond to His message, so He explained the story only to those who He knew wanted to understand? And then you realize His 12 chosen disciples were there, yet we know Judas would betray Him! Why did He explain the parable to Judas knowing that Judas would soon not follow Him? It doesn't seem fair to the multitude of people to which Jesus preached!

We know God is sovereign; He is God; and He did create us and has the right to shape us and use us as He wills.

> We also know, as written in Ephesians 1:9-14, "*and He made known to us the mystery of His will according to His good pleasure, which He purposed in Christ, to be put into effect when the times will have reached their fulfillment—to bring all things in heaven and earth together under one Head, even Christ. In Him we were chosen, having been predestined according to the plan of Him who works out everything in conformity with the purpose of His will, in order that we, who hope in Christ, might be for the praise of His glory. And you also were included in Christ when you heard the word of truth, the gospel of your salvation. Having believed, you were marked in Him with a seal, the promised Holy Spirit, who is a deposit guaranteeing our inheritance until the redemption of those who are God's possession, to the praise of His glory!*"

Did we choose to believe, or did God's grace become so irresistible that we could not say "NO" any longer?

This is a mystery! I cannot explain in detail how I came to believe, but I know this: for 46 years I did not believe, yet before I was 47 I did believe and God changed me totally and I praise Him every day and will forever! Is He done with me yet? Hardly! But I know this, each message that touches my heart changes me, and for the good. Therefore, I become more like Him all the time despite who I was in the past or who I am today!

Remember, there are 27 verses which talk about the mysteries of God. Read them soon, as I will list them at the end of this chapter for your home study. I want to focus on what we can understand and I can explain!

> Ephesians 3:4-6, "*In reading this, then, you will be able to understand my insight into the mystery of Christ, which was not made known to*

men in other generations as it has now been revealed by the Holy Spirit to God's holy apostles and prophets. This mystery is that through the gospel the gentiles are heirs together with Israel, members together of one body, and sharers together in the promise in Christ Jesus."

This verse was written 2000 years ago and is still true today. In today's world sin exists, yet we know by what has been written in the New Testament books, we are offered salvation in Christ, who is Jesus. And when, by faith, believers receive Christ, they also receive the Holy Spirit, which seals us until His return. We have Christian music, Christian TV programs, Bibles, Christian radio, cell phones, cable TV and all sorts of media that was not available when Scripture was written. Even so, for every one Christian based school, there are many more non-Christian options; TV channels at least 100 non-Christian to one Christian, and so it is with all options; the worldly views are shared and believed by more than those who become born again.

The mystery in Jesus is how can He be fully God and how can He at the same time be fully man? My best answer is this: "With God, all things are possible." The Bible says His grace is sufficient for us and that faith in Christ will result in eternal life. I'm not expected to explain the Creator; just believe in Him and let Him have His way with me. So I do!

I acknowledge that the Bible says I have a will of my own. I acknowledge the sovereignty of God. I know we have rights as believers, and I know that many are the plans of man, but it is the will of God that prevails. If you believe in free will, you believe the "free" part has no strings attached. Free from danger? NO. Free from discipline? NO. Free from death? NO. Free to live a private life? NO. Free from taxes? NO. So I ask this: What verses in the Bible declare our free will? Or is it a philosophy of man that reads into Scripture what they think could be there?

I believe every day brings many choices that we make, and that every one makes a difference in our lives. I wake up in the morning and decide: get up now or later? I choose, usually now, because I work. If I choose later, I'm late to work, so I may be disciplined by my boss. Too often and I may lose my job. If I lose my job, I lose my income, so I can't pay my bills, so I lose my car or my house or my wife! I eat poorly to save money and I get sick and I can't afford medicine, so I suffer longer, which made me miss a good job opportunity, which depresses me, which angers me, which drives me to drinking, which drives me to drugs, which cost money, so I steal and get caught, go to jail, lose my freedom, which makes me angrier, which leads to more depression, which leads to health issues, which means I can't even do my job any more, which is depressing, which leads me to more drinking and more drugs, which leads to more fines I can't afford to pay and I'm put back in jail! All because I chose to sleep in! So where does the "free" part of "free will" happen?

When you are born, you enter the world spiritually dead and slave to sin. If you receive Christ, you become a slave to righteousness. I agree Christ is eternally better, but either way, you are slave. Where's the "free" part? If you choose Christ as Lord, and He disciplines those He loves, who chooses when and how? Do you exercise your free will and become "free" from discipline? God chose when you would be born and when you will die. Can your "free" will change either one? Can you choose by free will to live alone somewhere and have total privacy? Or is God watching every moment, observing, reading your mind, searching your heart? If you have free will, you could hide at will, but you can't!

My point is this. We have freedoms; whether we are spiritually saved or unsaved; but God is above all! God allows choices, but good or bad choices will come at some cost. And the Bible teaches us to count the costs before we make the decision. Is free will a good thing or a curse? You decide. And is free a good way to describe the condition of humanity? Free will speaks of independence, and attracts many followers, who pridefully declare what they will do, where they will go, how things will be, and how tomorrow will be a better day.

God's will resists the proud but lifts up the humble. Those who give up and surrender their will and trust in His will, will prevail and become interdependent. Dependent wholly on Him, and then on the rest of the body, whose Head is Jesus. Like Jesus told His disciples to pray "Thy will be done on earth, as it is in heaven". Not my will; free or costly; but God's will. A mystery!

I'm not going to spend time talking about things that even the Bible tells us we won't understand. It is Satan who brings up issues that cause division, arguing, and tension between various parts of the body of Christ. You should read all of God's Word, including the verses on mysteries, and by faith, trust that God will reveal the truth about all things in His time. To love one another does not mean judge who is right or who is wrong; let God do that. Discern when to agree or disagree, and try not to be a stumbling block to others. And don't allow them to be a stumbling block to you either! Knowledge is good; wisdom is better.

Below is a list from my concordance on the topic of "Mysteries". If you are curious, look them up and see how many you can explain without conflict with other verses or beliefs. Matthew 13:11; Mark 4:11; Luke 8:10; Romans 11:25; Romans 16:25; 1 Corinthians 2:7; 1 Corinthians 4:1; 1 Corinthians 13:2; 1 Corinthians 14:2; 1 Corinthians 15:51; Ephesians 1:9; Ephesians 3:3; Ephesians 3:4; Ephesians 3:9; Ephesians 5:32; Ephesians 6:19; Colossians 1:26; Colossians 1:27; Colossians 2:2; Colossians 4:3; 2 Thessalonians 2:7; 1 Timothy 3:9; 1 Timothy 3:16; Revelations 1:20; Revelations 10:7; Revelations 17:7.

GOD'S MYSTERIES

What I don't understand is why I can't understand,
Why you can't understand what I understand to be true.
Is there something in me, that I cannot see, that you see in me?
When I see me doing what you see is wrong, yet I still do.

Can you help me explain, what I can't put in words, as I try to explain,
Why I can't explain, the things in my brain I can't explain.
How far can I go, if I don't know, if you want me to go,
Where I want to go, if I'm not sure if I want to go-should I remain?

If truth is revealed, then why am I sealed, and expected to surrender,
Though I've been set free, to slavery, that says die for those still dead.
If God chose me, before I could choose, though I wanted to choose Him,
What if I choose not to choose, what I know I should choose, even though
He chose me because He's the Head?

What would I see, if the Spirit in me, relied on me to see what I can't see,
Without the Spirit in me, showing me, what to see; would I be lost?
If my hearing is bad, will I hear what is good, or can't I hear what is good
Because my hearing is bad. Can you hear me? Can you hear the cost?

So do mysteries remain, to drive us insane, or do they force us to think,
What others think, which I think is wrong, but you think is right,
Which we both think is crazy, which we both think is not true,
Which makes us both think, our thinking is incomplete.

So we stumble and fall, and after it all, we realize grace, and fall on our face,
By faith we believe and obey and follow, a mystery even to me,
And yet I now see, how He uses me, in ways I can't explain,
And may remain, until the judgment seat, when we will meet.

I've never written a poem like this, if it is a poem at all? I did rhyme the last word of each thought, but forced you to think through each line, hoping you could see the mystery in each verse. I had fun writing it, even though many of you will miss the message it brings. I don't think we should doubt our understandings and thoughts, just be aware that God can work together for good all things to those who believe in Him. Love and obey; work together; make peace; mysteries are okay!

SPRING IS ALIVE

She comes each year to visit Libby; but not to stay,
She comes to warm our hearts; she melts the cold of winter away.
Her soft breeze and gentle rains, wake up our plants and flowers,
She inspires love; she draws us to herself; she entertains us for hours.

She knows no boundaries; she moves here and there; at her own pace,
She can be unpredictable at times; beauty in motion; hard to trace.
Her presence is felt by nature itself, and robins declare she is here,
She watches as new life appears; fawns, calves, and colts are near.

She brings us back to our fishing places, shortly after spawn,
She watches as our campfires glow; she hears us mow our lawns.
Her time has come and soon will leave, as summer takes her wing,
She isn't just alive and well; she is the one called Spring.

SPRING - 2010

March twenty of twenty ten, spring has finally come again.
A time; a season; with winter behind; of anticipation, of what we might find.

Not to say that all is good! Though Obama has bailed out all that he could,
And the housing market continues to fall, and signs of recession written on the wall.

Now that health insurance is offered to all, does that mean the cost of living will fall?
And as our jobs are harder to find, does that mean our taxes won't rob us all blind?

So as we ponder the newness of spring, is there peace in your soul, about anything?
Well, I'm glad that you asked me; I've good news to share,
The story of Easter and the cross we must bear.

Your hope is in Jesus; His blood shed for you, you need
to receive Him, to make all things new.
Rejoice in the springtime; find joy that will last, salvation is future, forgiving your past.

Forgive me for mixing the bad news and good, I'd make your decision, if only I could.
If life was all roses, we'd still find the thorn, to breath is not living; life is spiritually born.

FINDING JESUS

The world, and self, are always on a diet,
Though nothing works alone, you're still compelled to try it!
Too much weight, for eyes to see,
This isn't the person, I want to be!

But good news is coming, it will set you free,
The mystery is revealed in the recipe.
You eat all you want, the ingredients are free,
Your appearance will change, if you listen to me!

Now focus on Jesus; now don't that taste right!
Eat all you can handle, absorb day and night.
Your mind once resisted, but now you have Spirit,
The devil will tempt you, but your heart will not hear it!

Now don't you feel better? Your body looks great!
The Spirit, inside you, has lifted your weight!
The world will now notice; the wait brought a smile,
Yourself, now with Jesus, made this diet worthwhile.

If you lost what I promised, give this poem to a friend,
A prayer to thank Jesus, is all he will spend,
He died for our body, to make payment for sins,
When you ask for God's diet, your weight loss begins.

Chapter 13
CONCLUSION: THE END OF TIME IS NEAR

God lives in heaven where there are no clocks. The Bible teaches that to God, a thousand years are like a day, and a day is like a thousand years, which is to say, this thing called time has no meaning in heaven. God has always been. He is alive today, and He will be alive forever more. And at some point, He has appointed a moment when His true church will enter into His presence. We will be given glorified bodies that will never die, which will never experience pain of any kind; which will live and love forever with Him. This is His promise to those who come to believe in Him.

Time was introduced to man on earth so we could establish reference points in history and in our daily lives. Knowing that the clock is ticking and that time is running out, we have some measure of urgency in our lives to get done those things that are important to us, or for a few, important to God.

LIFE

On any given day, we all have 24 hours of time. For some, half of that time is spent sleeping, resting and keeping house. Then we eat 2 or 3 meals a day; say a total of 2 hours used up. Then we go to work, say 8 hours on a work day, plus eat up driving time, getting there early to beat the rush hour traffic, and driving home after a few minutes of talking; another hour gone, or more. So far, 23 hours used up and 1 hour left for the other activities in our life! Things like spiritual growth and fellowship, vacations, fishing, hunting, camping, phone calls, computer time, TV time, movies, etc!

Now that describes a normal workday. Most people only work for income 5 days a week, then have two days off. A typical Saturday is for fun stuff, and Sundays a day of rest, including sleeping in for some, or winding down a two day weekend and getting ready to do it over again!

My point is this: TIME FLIES! Time moves quickly and never comes back! You can store up extra vacation time at work by working overtime on a workday, but you give up an equal amount of time to get it! The more time spent on anything, the less time we have for something else!

So, since we've all been there, we make adjustments. We sleep less so we can work or play more. We multi-task, like talking on the phone, while we're watching football on TV, while we're eating a meal, while we're waiting for the car to warm up, so we can go enjoy something with our kids! While driving there, Dad complains about the traffic and listens to the football game on the radio; Mom vents what went wrong yesterday as she complains how loud the radio is. One kid is texting a message on his phone to Facebook because all of his friends are busy, and the other kid has his headphones on for privacy as he connects to the internet on his phone and looks at pictures of what his friends did last night for fun. Finally, you reach your destination, which is closed for remodeling. So you sit there and ask "What do we do now?"

Dad's mad at Mom for not calling ahead and making sure the place was open. Mom tells Dad that he's the one who wanted to go in the first place. Dad argues that he only wanted to go because Mom said we never go anywhere together. One kid is still texting on his phone and doesn't care where we go next. The other kid takes a picture of the closed place with his phone, posts it on Facebook, and tells everybody not to go there. When Mom asks the first one where he wants to go, he doesn't answer, since his headphones are still on playing music. We don't have time to drive so far to the next place, so we drive home and say we'll do it again some other time!

So in our short description of events, a week has gone by! We take our paycheck and pay bills and hope our heating bill is less next month. We complain about the two hundred bucks we spend at the phone company. After all, Dad doesn't answer his phone; Mom carries hers in her purse, but nobody calls her; one kid only does texting and one kid only puts pictures on Facebook, and if he does call someone, it's usually Mom to get a ride somewhere. We pay the cable bill, complaining that we never watch 395 channels of the 400 we pay for! We pay our house insurance, our car insurance, our truck insurance, our boat insurance, our camper insurance and our medical insurance; all of which have a $1000 deductible, so we hope we never need it! We have other bills, so we put them on a new credit card because it offers 2 years interest free. We pay our car payment, but see that it's cheaper to buy a new car than to make the payment on our old car, so we buy a new one for no money down, no interest for 7 years, and they will even finance the $5,000 we would lose on our trade in! When the new insurance bill comes in, we realize our bill doubled!

We pay our house payment, and wish there wasn't 20 years left on our mortgage. Then we see a statement saying "Refinance today at a lower rate, no out of pocket closing costs plus get extra money for stuff you've always wanted". So we make a call, get approved and sign papers, what a deal! Six months later, we wish we didn't have 40 years left on our home mortgage, instead of 20! Five years go by, and our kids graduate and move out of the house. We decide to downsize, so we proceed to sell the house. The economy took a turn for the worse, and our house is worth $20,000 less than what we owe! We can't sell! Retirement age comes, but we can't afford to retire! Mom and Dad die and the mortgage company takes the house. The bank takes the car. The kids pay for the funeral and everyone on Facebook feels bad that they didn't have more time to enjoy their life with family and friends.

In our sadly believable story, did you notice something missing? No one took the time to spend it with God! They didn't go to Sunday school or church, and if they did from time to time, it never changed their lives. Tithing, gifts and offerings were not in their budget! And in the end, they had nothing to take with them except what they were born with: their sin nature, which separated them from God; which carried with it a penalty for sin, which is death! Eternal separation from God in a place called hell. Death, the one spiritual present we all inherit from our forefathers, which most people bring to their grave! The Bible says there is death, and then a second death.

Spiritual death is to be separated from God. Sin causes death. Since all people have sinned, all people fall short of the glory of God.

> In Revelation 21:8, the Bible says, *"But the cowardly, the unbelieving, the vile, the murderers, and sexually immoral, those who practice magic arts, the idolaters and all liars – their place will be in the fiery lake of burning sulfur. This is the second death."*

You are born with your sin nature, and are spiritually dead. If you come to Jesus and make peace with God, He will give you eternal life. If you don't come to Christ, your second death experience will last forever and nothing will ever give you comfort!

So how will we know when the end days the Bible talks about are near? The Bible gives us good insight, so that we may at least know the season – winter, spring, summer...... and then the fall!

One event: the rapture, will remove those in Christ.
> In Matthew 24:30, the Bible says, *"At that time the sign of the Son of Man will appear in the sky, and all the nations of the earth will mourn. They will see the Son of Man coming on the clouds of the sky, with power and great glory. And He will send His angels with a loud trumpet call, and they will gather His elect from the four winds, from one end of the heavens to the other."*
> The warning is BE READY!

> Another warning: 1 Peter 4:7 says, *"The end of all things is near."*

Live your life urgently and with the mindset that perhaps His return is today!
> In Acts 1:7, Jesus says, *"It is not for you to know the times or dates the Father has set by His own authority."*

You are to believe He is coming back, and you are to be ready.

> 2 Timothy 3:1-5 says, *"But mark this: there will be terrible times in the last days. People will be lovers of themselves, lovers of money, boastful, proud, abusive, disobedient to their parents, ungrateful, unholy, without love, unforgiving, slanderous, without self-control, brutal, not lovers of good, treacherous, rash, conceited, lovers of pleasure rather than lovers of God – having a form of godliness but denying its power."* Plus a warning, *"Have nothing to do with them."*

We have studied Scripture and have discussed the fruits of the Holy Spirit in true believers: love, joy, peace, patience, kindness, gentleness, faithfulness and self-control. In the final days, the people with sinful hearts will outnumber believers by a great number! They will be the majority, and will control lawmakers, law enforcers and change how we live. Fear will be a daily threat, violence will be everywhere. Worldly people will love their lives. They will eat, drink, and be merry! They will be proud of what they have accomplished, and pay no attention to God, in church, in home life, or in community events. Every day is about having a good time! If you have time, watch tonight's news and listen for hints of violence, brutality or abuses. Any shootings today? What sports millionaire got arrested in a late night bar fight during a moment of rage? Who bombed who this week?

> In Matthew 24:1-5, the disciples ask Jesus when the end will come, and Jesus gave this warning in verses 6-14: *"You will hear of wars and rumors of wars, but see to it that you are not alarmed. Such things must happen, but the end is still to come. Nation will rise against nation, and kingdom against kingdom. There will be famines and earthquakes in various places. All these are the beginning of birth pains. Then you will be handed over to be persecuted and put to death, and you will be hated by all nations because of Me. At that time many will turn away from the faith and will betray and hate each other, and many false prophets will appear and deceive many people. Because of the increase of wickedness, the love of most will grow cold, but he who stands firm to the end will be saved. And this gospel of the kingdom of God will be preached in the whole world as a testimony to all nations, and then the end will come."*

So there you have a clear picture of the last days and also the end. You make your own mind up! Answer these few questions---

1. Are there wars or rumors of wars? Yes or No
2. Is Israel in the news lately? Yes or No
3. Any diseases? Earthquakes? Volcanoes? Floods? Yes or No

4. Anyone on the news lost their head lately? Yes or No
5. Any divorces? Suicides? Rapes? Murders? Yes or No
6. Any false prophets or TV evangelists asking for money? Yes or No
7. Despite danger and corruption – Is God's Word reaching the world? Yes or No

If you can see these things happening, the end is near. Consider all the warnings we looked at, and if you think it over, you can form an opinion as to how close we are. As for me, I say any day! Be watching UPWARD!

> One closing Scripture: Luke 21:25-28. Jesus says, *"There will be signs in the sun, moon and stars. On the earth, nations will be in anguish and perplexity at the roaring and tossing of the sea. Men will faint from terror, apprehensive of what is coming on the world, for the heavenly bodies will be shaken. At that time they will see the Son of Man coming in a cloud with power and great glory. When these things begin to take place, stand up and lift your head, because your redemption is drawing near."*

Bottom line – Jesus is coming back; soon, quickly, justly! Believers caught up; non-believers cut down. And when the church is gone, His light is gone; and darkness will remain with one guarantee left: 7 years of tribulation, while the promised judgments of God come to the world and those left behind.

Don't be left behind! Make peace with God today! Tomorrow may not come to you! And when the last day comes, it's coming for you – READY OR NOT!

TIME - - OR NOT!

On earth; we take pleasure; in things we can measure; yet time slips away.
In heaven; eternal; or hellish infernal; eternally only one day.

On earth; we are born; we're happy or mourn; then comes the end of me.
In heaven; we arrive; we're already alive; and we always will be.

On earth; there is war and sins that we die for; that time cannot heal.
In heaven; always peace, only right; only more; joy is all we feel.

On earth; much disgrace; with tears on our face; a time of disaster.
In heaven; delight; for He is our light; praising our Master.

On earth; time is short; women abort; and time costs you money.
In heaven; forever no wronging; children belonging; and money is funny.

On earth; you decide; it's a matter of pride; your time can be bold.
In heaven; Jesus will reign; His word will remain; His streets are of gold.

On earth; fear will stay; until the final day; then time is a chore.
In heaven; love will prevail; our King we will hail; forever more.

ALMOST THERE

Hide me in You, Jesus, as Your purpose is revealed.
Guide me in the process, as Your will in me is sealed.
Show me love and patience, as we do the things You've planned.
Discipline as needed, as you hold me in Your hand.

Change is surely needed, as I long to be like You.
Heart and mind amended, by the things You say and do.
Teach me ways I'm missing, so I stay upon Your path.
I love this life You've given, as You saved me from Your wrath.

So in the days before me, give me grace as I obey.
Gently draw me to You, in the moments that I stray.
Not by good intentions, but by faith I want to live.
Not by things acquired, but by ways I've learned to give.

In the end times that we live in, may we trust You even more.
Focusing on heaven, and the things You have in store.
Keep us from temptation, as we strive to do what's right.
Fuel the light within us, every morning, day and night.

ABOUT THE AUTHOR

In 1996 I became a born again follower of Jesus Christ. In 1997 I went on my first 3 week mission trip, which led me to Libby, Montana to attend a missionary school known as International Messengers. Eighteen years later and I'm still in Libby! Though most of my ministries involve work outside the walls of our local church, I continue to minister to our youth, as well as sharing Christ weekly at the Lincoln County Jail.

Though I enjoy the work the Lord has called me to, I've wanted for a long time to be able to spend time on a book that would take Scriptures and organize them in a way that the lost or deceived could come to an understanding of what God has done for all of us, and how it is God's hope that all would be saved. Many people these days are too busy to read the Bible, and therefore never come to realize what God has planned for their lives! Now 65 and retired, I have the time to share with all who seek truth, and hopefully, many will come to know Jesus through His Word and the gifts shared in this book.

My wife, Bonnie and I are currently in the fundraising process for a mission trip to Antigua, Guatemala in February 2016. Our local fellowship, Faith Bible Church, has a team of 9 members joining with Three Crosses Church of Spokane, Washington, to bring and install water filters in local homes with dirty water. In addition, we will be bringing bi-lingual Bibles and Spanish children's books to hand out at local schools and orphanages. Our hope is that the Lord will use us to draw many to Jesus during our time there, and that our lives will be changed as we minister to their needs. If you, the reader, is willing, pray for all of us; for health, unity and faithfulness to the One we serve.